Confronting Anti-Semitism
A Practical Guide

Confronting Anti-Semitism
A Practical Guide

by

Leonard P. Zakim

edited by
Janice Ditchek

KTAV Publishing House, Inc.
Hoboken, New Jersey

Library of Congress Cataloging-in-Publication Data

Zakim, Leonard P.
          Confronting anti-semitism: a practical guide / by Leonard P. Zakim: edited
    by Janice Ditchek.
          p. cm.
       Includes bibliographical references.
       ISBN 0-88125-629-3 (ppk)   0-88125-674-9 (cloth)
           1. Antisemitism - United States. 2. Afro-Americans - Relations with Jews.
           3. United States - Ethnic relations. I. Ditchek, Janice

II. Title.
DS146.U6Z35 1999
305.892.4073 - dc 21

                                                                98-54982
                                                                CIP

Manufactured in the United States
Distributed by
KTAV Publishing House, Inc.
900 Jefferson St.
Hoboken, NJ 07030

Table of Contents

• **Acknowledgments** . . . . **xi**

• **Foreword** . . . . **xv**

• **Introduction** . . . . **xix**

• **Why Respond?** **1**
This chapter presents a rationale for a tactical and informed response by all who are concerned about the impact of anti-Semitism.

• **How Do We Respond: Strategic Guidelines** **5**
This chapter provides generic strategies for responding to anti-Semitism.

• **The Myths** **12**
This chapter provides examples and suggested responses to anti-Semitic myths that continue to find currency in both public and private discourse today. The myths explored in this book are:

   "They killed Jesus"
   "They poison our wells"
   "They control the money"
   "They're cheap"
   "They conspire to control the world"
   "Their national loyalty can't be trusted"
   "The Holocaust didn't happen"
   "They had a major role in the slave trade"
   "The Hamitic Myth"

• **Confronting Anti-Semitism on a Personal Level . . . 43**
This chapter suggests strategies for response when confronted by anti-Semitism among acquaintances and in everyday situations.

• **Coalition Building** **52**
This chapter demonstrates the importance of strong and positive coalitions in the fight against anti-Semitism and tells how to build and sustain them.

• **Finding Someone To Blame: The Anatomy of Anti-Semitism** **60**
by Dr. Leon Jick

• **Anti-Semitism and Black-Jewish Relations** **67**
by Jonathan Kaufman

• **Anti-Judaism, Anti-Semitism: History, Roots, and Cures** **82**
by Dr. Padraic O'Hare

• **Definitions of Anti-Semitism** **109**

• **Denominational Statements Against Anti-Semitism** **113**

• **Denominational Statements on the Holocaust** **116**

• **Notes** **148**

• **Bibliography** **157**

WHY RESPOND

HOW DO WE RESPOND

THE MYTHS

ANTI-SEMITISM: KNOW HOW TO RESPOND

"FINDING SOMEONE TO BLAME"

"THEOLOGICAL ROOTS OF ANTI-SEMITISM"

ANTI-SEMITISM

The tendency to think of Jews in terms of negative imagery and beliefs which lead one to see them as power hungry, materialistic, aggressive, dishonest, or clannish…the willingness to shun Jews, speak ill of them, subject them to social discrimination, or deny them social and legal rights afforded to society's non-Jews on the basis of a belief that Jews must be treated differently because they are different, alien and malevolent.[1]

Anti-Semitism: know how to respond

Acknowledgments

This book was written with a great deal of help from many people. I wish to thank Beth and Gerald Tischler for their generous financial support, which made the research for this book possible; Abraham Foxman for his belief in this endeavor and the institutional support he provided; Pearl Tendler Mattenson for her coordination of the initial phase of this project and for her assistance throughout; Sarit Sapir for her early research assistance; Tom Kaminsky for his assistance on graphic design; Jonathan Kaufman, Professor Padraic O'Hare, and Professor Leon Jick for their eloquent contributions; Debbie Cox, Brenda Jones, and Stacey Maher for their technical support; Kenneth Jacobson for his support and insightful comments on the text; Alan Schwartz and David Cantor for reading and providing counsel on sections of the manuscript; Gail Gans, for reviewing the text and her much valued research assistance, and my many colleagues in the field who devote themselves to the mission and goals of ADL and strive daily to stop all forms of bigotry. I am also grateful to Larry Sternberg and Professor Stephen Whitfield of Brandeis University for reviewing and commenting on the text in its earliest stages. Finally, I wish to express special gratitude to my friend, associate, colleague, and editor, Janice Ditchek, for her shared commitment and enthusiasm for this project and all that it represents.

Dedication

To every person who has encountered the pain of anti-Semitism and will now, with this book as a guide, be empowered to confront it.

To my family—my wife Joyce, for her support of my work all these years, and her strength and caring, and to my children and all children, who I hope will someday live in a world without hatred of Jews or any other group.

Foreword

Leo Frank at his Trial in 1913.

In assessing anti-Semitism at the end of the twentieth century, one must first acknowledge how far the Jewish people have come on the road to acceptance and achievement. One hundred years ago, millions of Jews fled Czarist pogroms and poverty in Eastern Europe to come to the United States. Here, though finding refuge and the chance for a better life, they faced systemic, legally sanctioned discrimination, popular ridicule, and cruel stereotypes. In 1913, a group of concerned Jews established the Anti-Defamation League to facilitate Jewish participation in American life, and to call on this nation to live up to its promise of liberty, justice, and fair treatment for all citizens.

The first event that compelled the ADL's attention was the outrageous case of Leo Frank, a Georgia businessman held for a murder he plainly had not committed, convicted and sentenced to death amid a blatantly anti-Semitic atmosphere. After Georgia's governor commuted the sentence to life in prison, and despite a national campaign spearheaded by leading public figures to free him, Frank was kidnapped from prison and lynched in 1915.

In the 1920s, the Ku Klux Klan attracted nearly five million men to an ideology of anti Semitism, racism, xenophobia, and terrorism, while Congress was unable to pass a national law against lynching. In the 1930s, one of the most popular political commentators on the radio was the rabidly anti-Jewish priest, Father Charles Coughlin. At the outset of World War II, a pro-Nazi German-American Bund claimed thousands of members, and Jews were routinely beaten on the streets of Philadelphia, New York, and Boston by anti-Semitic street gangs. (Needless to say, this was not the worst fate to befall Jews during World War II.)

At the same time, however, other trends began to change in America. The ridicule of Jews in the popular media progressively diminished, though it has never entirely disappeared. Newspaper editors, spurred by a campaign coordinated by ADL, discontinued the practice of identifying criminal suspects by their religion or ethnicity. These trends coincided with the growing integration of Jews into the mainstream of American life.

In the two decades following World War II, a new spirit awakened in America. Veterans, particularly Black veterans, returned from fighting against Hitler's unprecedented bigotry and found the American segregation and Jim Crow laws alive and well. American resistance to integration and the deprivation of fundamental civil rights served as a catalyst for a grassroots movement for equality. Sensitized by the spectre of the Holocaust, Jews joined African-Americans and others to invigorate a civil rights movement that slowly changed America through political, social and legislative reform.

In contrast to the days of Father Coughlin, a spirit of ecumenism characterizes the relationship of Judaism to other religions in the United States today. The hate groups that once claimed thousands, even millions of members lie in disrepute and disarray. Although those that remain constitute a serious, sometimes deadly threat to the safety and security of minorities throughout the country, the contribution of Jews to virtually all walks of life in America is nevertheless significant and largely unfettered.

Why, then, does ADL continue in its mission to alert the public to the dangers of anti Semitism? Why, in the words of our critics, do we react even to the smallest flickerings of bigotry? The answer is simple, but too easily dismissed: even wide-ranging success in countering and reducing prejudice cannot provide the "magic bullet" cure; we have not found a foolproof antidote to the virus of hate.

Organized hate groups may be small and isolated, but even a few fanatics are still capable of serious violence - the Oklahoma City and World Trade Center catastrophes prove that. The internet also has provided haters with unexpected new propaganda and recruitment opportunities. Yes, many polls have indicated a steady drop in anti-Semitic attitudes and the readiness of most Americans to work with, live among, and vote for their Jewish fellow citizens. But an ADL national survey in 1998 found that 20 to 25 million Americans harbor some anti-Jewish attitudes, including accusations of "dual loyalty" and "control" of financial and political institutions. Minister Louis Farrakhan's demagogic tirades elicit applause and approval from audiences of thousands. Ads promoting Holocaust denial have appeared in dozens of campus newspapers.

Silence and complacency would only allow this poison to proliferate. We may have learned to anticipate and control the spread of anti-Semitism - but you don't shut down the fire department just because the latest arson has been put out.

Vigilance remains our crucial responsibility. Education - especially of the young - to combat the corrosive effects of ignorance, scapegoating, and stereotyping is our ongoing duty to history, to Jewish security, and to democratic values. This book plays a critical role toward fulfilling these commitments.

It provides:

- an examination of anti-Semitic ideas that have prompted anti-Semitic acts for two thousand years.
- the historical background of these ideas - where they come from, and what image of Jews or Judaism they invoke.
- strategies for counteracting them in a constructive manner.

By alerting readers to the misinformation and faulty reasoning of such ideas, *Confronting Anti-Semitism* makes an important contribution toward enabling them to respond effectively should they encounter anti-Semitism on the street, in the classroom, or among peers. Reason alone is not always sufficient to counter unreason and hate, but logic and knowledge can often provide a means of ensuring that the home Jews have found in America continues to be safe and open to all.

Abraham H. Foxman Howard P. Berkowitz
National Director   National Chairman
Anti-Defamation League

Introduction

Most people know about the anti-Semitism that resulted in the murder of six million Jews during the Holocaust. The news media, history books, television shows, films and popular literature have educated many of us to the traumatic impact of anti-Semitism and other forms of hate in society today. But few words have been written, or broadcasts aired, to prepare people to take action when anti-Semitism occurs.

Ill-equipped to respond, some of us shrink from direct intervention and rebuttal when confronted with anti-Semitism. Others react, but meekly and ineffectively. And oftentimes, those who do reply assertively lack the necessary factual armor.

It is to provide the essential factual and strategic information that this book has been written. Indeed, its very origin is rooted in the confessed inability of Jews and non-Jews to refute anti-Semitism in all its manifestations. More specifically, this book is intended to serve as a guide to provide both historical and current context to the most commonly heard anti-Semitic myths. Of equal importance, it is designed as a tool for those who without these practical steps would be left to react in silence.

The need to meet this challenge is not new. It has plagued Jews and other opponents of anti-Semitism for decades, if not centuries. And, as those who have turned the corner from inaction to action can attest, the results can be significant.

Consider one young person's experience:

A thirteen-year-old boy in Wayne, New Jersey, was speechless and without a clue as to how to react the first time he was called a kike by a "friend."

> *"LIKE THE HERO OF THAT NOVEL (The Trial) THE JEW IS ENGAGED IN A LONG TRIAL. HE DOES NOT KNOW HIS JUDGES, SCARCELY EVEN HIS LAWYERS, HE DOES NOT KNOW WHAT HE IS CHARGED WITH, YET HE KNOWS THAT HE IS CONSIDERED GUILTY."*
>
> **JEAN-PAUL SARTRE**

When that same boy stooped to pick a penny off the ground at the school yard, he was jeered by classmates who called him a "cheap Jew." Still not knowing how best to respond, he stood by, astonished and embarrassed.

A few years later, in high school, he had gained enough confidence and, unfortunately, enough experience as a target of anti-Semitism to muster a reply. So, when told by peers on numerous occasions that he wasn't like other Jews, he quickly retorted, "How many other Jews do you know?" Surprised by the question, most would stop, think, and quite often realize the absurdity of their comment before answering that, in fact, he was the only Jew they knew.

In law school, when he and a Jewish classmate successfully negotiated a substantial fee reduction for a benefit run by the student bar association, the incoming bar association president exclaimed, "Hey, you really 'jewed' him down!" Stunned by the insult, the young man admonished his peer for the anti-Semitic remark. The response triggered a lengthy discussion, and a professed understanding on the part of the offender as to why such a comment is anti-Semitic and hurtful.

That young Jewish person was me. After twenty years of working for the Anti-Defamation League, a premier American human-relations organization, I am finding that there exists yet another generation of young people, parents, and non-Jewish allies who are offended, hurt, and stymied by anti-Semitic remarks and incidents.

I did not really know how best to respond when I was a youth; but I knew from the examples set by my childhood heroes, such as Robert Kennedy and Dr. Martin Luther King, Jr., that a response to hate was necessary, and therefore responded instinctively.

Admittedly, what I experienced and others continue to face today is significantly different from the anti-Semitism that our parents and grandparents confronted before us. Even the most disturbing examples of anti-Semitism in my youth pale in comparison to the dehumanizing, institutional, and virulent anti-Semitism of prewar and wartime Europe which made the Holocaust possible.

The anti-Semitism we confront today is not the economically and theologically based anti-Semitism that was so brutally imposed on Europe's Jews for centuries prior to Auschwitz. Nor was it the contempt for Jews perpetuated or tolerated by the Catholic and Protestant Church or other Christian denominations. This contempt for Jews is rooted in the distorted interpretation of Matthew 27:25 "His blood be on us and our children" and reinforced through other anti-Jewish components of the Gospels. (See *Anti-Judaism, Anti-Semitism: History, Roots, and Cures* by Padraic O'Hare).

Often this hatred and hostility translated into violent and deadly anti-Semitic pogroms against local Jewish communities in Europe. Encouraged by the diminution of the humanity of individual Jews through sermons based on these Gospels and other anti-Semitic myths, the reaction to such violence was either complicity or apathy.

In America, the "Christ-killing" charge was uttered in schoolyards and repeated to millions of radio listeners by people like the "hate-priest" Father Charles Coughlin. It also manifested itself in brutal physical attacks on Jewish youths by Catholic teens in Boston, Chicago, New York and in other urban areas in the 30s and 40s. In the "bible belt," in parts of the South and Mid-West, anti-Semitic myths espoused by numerous Christian leaders translated into isolation and anti-Semitic harassment of numbers of Jews. The Klan and other extremist groups cited the deicide charge in their literature and used it in anti-Semitic diatribes at cross burning rallies.

We now live in a time when Cardinal Bernard Law of Boston and his fellow cardinals in Europe and North America have publicly declared that "Anti-Semitism is inconsistent with Christianity." [2] It is also a time in which Pope John Paul II has personally called the Jews "beloved brethren" and "older brothers" and has condemned the "hatred, persecutions and the manifestations of anti-Semitism perpetuated against the Jews at any time and by any person." Many Protestants and other Christian denominations have forcefully condemned anti-Semitism. Jews are not alone as much as they once were. They do have allies.

Yet, even in the early months of 1999 anti-Semitism proved that eulogies for its demise were unfortunately too early. Reverend Jerry Falwell, leader of the Moral Majority and a well-known Christian evangelical preacher warned that the coming anti-Christ would be a Jewish male. Former Ku Klux Klan leader David Duke released a new book, *My Awakening* promoting anti-Semitism and white supremacist views. The majority leader of the U.S. Senate, Trent Lott

"THE SPOILED SEEDS OF ANTI-JUDAISM AND ANTI-SEMITISM MUST NEVER AGAIN BE ALLOWED TO TAKE ROOT IN ANY HUMAN HEART."

HOLY SEE'S COMMISSION FOR RELIGIOUS RELATIONS WITH THE JEWS MARCH 1998

spoke before an audience of the Council of Conservative Citizens, a racist organization. Upon exposure of this association, Lott condemned the group as did prominent GOP Congressman Bob Barr of Georgia who also appeared before the organization.

In Europe as well, particularly in the former Soviet Union, Jews have once again become an increasingly popular scapegoat for Russia's many crises. Some prominent Russian political leaders openly engage in anti-Semitism, while others simply ignore anti-Jewish rhetoric spewed by their peers. Albert Makashov, a Communist leader in the Russian parliament, called in October 1998 for Jews to be rounded up and sent to the grave. A motion in the Russian Duma to condemn Makashov for his anti-Semitic threat and subsequently others was quashed and never came to a vote.

Anti-Semitism is included in Russian political party charters and is, according to *Time* Magazine reporter Andrew Meier, "the stuff of polite daily conversation in buses, kitchens and...bank lines." Media reports from Russian and from Jewish and other human rights organizations are documenting a myriad of incidents of anti-Semitic demagoguery, vandalism, scapegoating and periodic bomb attacks on Jewish synagogues. Charges of Jewish orchestrated genocide against the Russian people and Jewish control of the Russian press, government and banks are commonplace.

Anti-Semitism's contemporary manifestations reflect a kind of plagiarism from its old masters. In 1999, anti-Semitism ranges widely from attitudinal hate to the fears and fantasies of international Jewish conspiracies shared by White Christian leaders like Pat Robertson and African-American demagogues like Louis Farrakhan and Khalid Muhammad. In their wake is the paranoia of militia groups, local right-wing fringe groups, and local Nation of Islam chapters that exploit their particular brand of hate. Nation of Islam spokesmen parrot almost word for word text from Martin Luther's centuries-old anti-Semitic tract called the *Jews and their Lies*. The Lutheran church, however, rejected the blatant anti-Semitism of its founder. On April 18, 1994 the Church Council of the Evangelical Lutheran Church in America, adopted the following document as a statement on Lutheran-Jewish relations:

In the spirit of that truth-telling, we who bear his name and heritage must with pain acknowledge also Luther's anti-Judaic diatribes and violent recommendations of his later writings against the Jews. We particularly deplore the appropriation of Luther's words by modern anti-Semites for the teaching of hatred toward Judaism or toward the Jewish people in our day. We recognize in anti-Semitism a contradiction and an affront to the Gospel, a violation of our hope and calling, and we pledge this church to oppose the deadly working of such bigotry.

Anti-Semitic vandalism at synagogue in Phoenix, Arizona.

International Jewish conspiracy views provoke and sustain ancient hatreds, stereotyping, and distrust of Jews. Their roots lie in the forgery of a document called the *Protocols of the Learned Elders of Zion*. Although centuries' old charges of well poisoning, ritual slaughter of Christian children, perversion, and deicide preceded the *Protocols*, the document was widely distributed in the past and continues to fuel the anti-Semitism generated today in parts of the Arab press, by the Nation of Islam, and other extremist groups. In the winter of 1998, Iraq's dictator Sadaam Hussein blamed U.S. policy toward Iraq on a "Zionist clique" surrounding President Bill Clinton. Iraq had violated numerous U.N. resolutions and had been ostracized and criticized by its Arab neighbors for those acts as well.

As Richard Levy notes in Benjamin Segel's book, *A Lie and a Libel*, the *Protocols* depicts "a 2,000-year old, arcanely elaborate Jewish conspiracy possessed of an astounding intelligence network directed by a committee of nameless, bloodthirsty individuals immune to every decent human impulse."[3] Benjamin Segel opines that the anti-Semitism of the *Protocols* solves no real problems, but has "demonstrated the capacity to poison political life."[4] Such is the case today in America, the former Soviet Union, Malaysia, the Palestinian Authority and elsewhere where the *Protocols* are distributed.

The gradual process of intellectually accepting popularly-articulated theories of hate, distorted and falsified histories, and easy answers to complicated problems is a dangerous course. Whether promoted from a pulpit or a lectern, the continued promotion of hateful ideology leads to active aggression, mildly passive rejection, or a flat-out "look the other way" mentality. It is a process that must be stopped in its tracks.

Anti-Semites come in all shapes and sizes—in this way they are the same as other bigots. Irrationality is their mind set. To them, Jews have represented a supernatural, timeless image of evil: a greedy, whining, and complaining people; a population to be feared, suspected, despised, and guarded against for all sorts of perceived crimes and innately negative characteristics. This variety of anti-Semitic imagery further confuses those who would condemn the acts of neo-Nazi skinheads, synagogue and cemetery desecrations, but refuse to resign from a club that doesn't admit Jews as members or to speak out when an anti-Semitic "joke" is told.

Even today, one does not need to look hard to find anti-Semitism. In Germany, according to a December 1998 op-ed in the *New York Times*, accusations abound calling attorneys seeking restitution for Holocaust survivors and their families "money grubbing Jewish lawyers."[5] In Switzerland, following the shocking disclosure in 1996 of the Swiss banks' collaboration with Nazi confiscation of Jewish properties and money, government officials warned Jews not to be too aggressive about the issue lest it provoke anti-Semitism.

Like cancer, anti-Semitism cannot wait to be taken seriously only after violent symptoms occur. Early evidence of the disease must be exposed and combatted. The pain that anti-Semitism inflicts, psychologically as well as physically, must be acknowledged, and its targets and victims attended to with sensitivity and practical measures. Victims and targets of anti-Semitism need to know they have allies.

In recent years, as Jews in America have gained acceptance into far-reaching echelons of professional and public life, anti-Semitism has been increasingly couched in "polite" forms of stereotyping rather than the blatant attacks of the past. This shift, no matter how dramatic, should not be confused with anti-Semitism's elimination. As Mark Twain once wrote: "The reports of my death are greatly exaggerated." So too, even in the late 1990s, are the oft-written obituaries for anti-Semitism. The fact that American anti-Semitism today is not as deep-seated and routinely poisonous as racism must not be falsely embraced as the end of the problem itself.

Nevertheless, there has been real progress. Advances in the fight against anti-Semitism are commonly reflected by

> "ANTI-SEMITISM HAS ALWAYS BEEN THE CHEAPEST MEANS EMPLOYED BY SELFISH MINORITIES FOR DECEIVING THE PEOPLE. A TYRANNY BASED ON SUCH DECEPTION AND MAINTAINED BY TERROR MUST INEVITABLY PERISH FROM THE POISON IT GENERATES WITHIN ITSELF."
>
> ALBERT EINSTEIN

swift official responses to hate crimes; more effective prosecutions of the illegal acts of extremist groups; and a noticeable reduction in the traditional measures of anti-Semitic stereotyping, exclusion, and discrimination. The success of meaningful and honest interfaith alliances against anti-Semitism with the Catholic Church and many Protestant denominations have proven to be enormously helpful. Anti-Semitism in U.S. politics, once commonplace, is now infrequent and increasingly unacceptable. A recent public opinion poll commissioned by the ADL documents a significant reduction in anti-Semitic attitudes among most American groups. This is progress that was well fought for and needs to be celebrated to reinforce that change is possible.[6]

More than anything else, an effective fight against anti-Semitism requires a resolute willingness to acknowledge that our efforts to combat it—both past and present, large and small—do make a difference. This acknowledgment should not diminish our energies against anti-Semitism or our awareness of it. Rather, it should fuel our collective communal commitment to take its measure and to strategically confront it for what it is today. It should give us hope for further success.

Today, as in the past, it is extremists on the right and the left who create a role and choice for people in the middle. One can be held hostage to their extremist views because confronting them takes knowledge and risk. One can choose to be comfortably ensconced in the so-called neutral zone, rebutting only the most obvious examples of anti-Semitism to consider the job complete. Or, to be truly effective, one can become educated about the historical facts behind the anti-Semitic myths, lies, and stereotypes. One can arm him- or herself with responses to refute them. That education must include a strategic analysis and plan of how to effectively respond to and mobilize others against anti-Semitism. This book provides a blueprint for both.

In this era of the information superhighway and media-driven politics, nothing short of the latter effort will suffice. Action against anti-Semitism starts with individuals willing to challenge it, protest it, and interrupt it.

Let us be careful to remember: Anti-Semitism has frequently been opposed and often, with success. Thousands of righteous Gentiles risked their lives to harbor Jews during the Holocaust. Émile Zola, in his classic essay, *J'accuse*, attacked

French anti-Semitism during the Dreyfus trial. Dr. Martin Luther King, Jr., opposed the anti-Semitism of some Black nationalists and others in his community with uncompromising intolerance, rhetorical vigor, and eloquence. Harvard University Chairman of Afro-American Studies, Henry Louis Gates, author Alice Walker, Congressman John Lewis and NAACP Chairman, Julian Bond among others, have vigorously exposed and condemned the anti-Semitism of Louis Farrakhan and the anti-Semitic publications of the Nation of Islam. The people of Billings, Montana set a national example in December 1993 of how non-Jews can react to anti-Semitism when most of its residents displayed menorahs in their windows to protest anti-Semitic vandalism during Hanukah. This community wide mobilization isolated the perpetrators and sent a strong message of support to the Jewish community.

In a lengthy and well-reasoned essay on anti-Semitism by the American conservative icon, William F. Buckley, he admitted that he could not defend his friend, Patrick Buchanan, against the charge of anti-Semitism. That admission took the burden off Jewish leaders and some Jewish columnists of having to prove the truth of that assertion. Buchanan's advocacy of the Reagan visit to Bitburg, Germany, a cemetery that included graves of S.S. members; flirtations with Holocaust deniers; attacks on American Jews for alleged "dual loyalty;" and his one-sided assaults on Israel were too much for Buckley to ignore. Buckley's essay was later published as a book titled, *In Search of Anti-Semitism*.

Anti-Semitism, it is true, has more often provoked indifference than resistance. The illusion of a "neutral bystander" in the face of such hostility, from those who looked on as Jewish homes were looted by Nazis to those who applaud, or ignore, or defend anti-Semitic speeches which they would never make themselves, and to those who laugh among their peers at anti-Jewish jokes, must be stripped away. Embarrassment by friends or colleagues at anti-Semitism without a clear rejection of it is still a form of harmful complicity—it is not neutrality.

Sometimes resistance to anti-Semitism is manifested in the personal touch: a smile or a word of welcome to an isolated new classmate at a formerly "exclusive" private school or club. It might take the form of an op-ed article in the organizational newsletter rebutting an anti-Semitic conspiracy theory overheard in the office cafeteria. It could be reflected in verbal support of a Jewish target of anti-Semitism, as in Billings, Montana, instead of leaving the victim to fend on his or her own.

It is towards this end that the information included in this book will be critical. In classrooms, in boardrooms, living rooms, and elsewhere, polite as well as demagogic anti-Semitism can be rebutted with the facts and strategies included in this volume. But it will also take a willingness to act.

History has taught us that Jews and their allies in other communities do not have the luxury of ignoring anti-Semitism. The risks of silence are too high and historically, the pain has been too deep to sit by and do nothing. As we have seen with the November 4, 1995 assassination of Israel's Prime Minister, Yitzhak Rabin, words of hate—unrebutted, ignored, or tolerated—can swiftly turn into actions of violence.

That's why the sometimes uncomfortable task of confronting anti-Semitism at every level continues to be imposed on us. It cannot be overemphasized that only the haters prosper when apathy or cowardice greets their words and deeds. If anti-Semites, like racists and other bigots, are not persistently and effectively challenged, they will not fade away. If anti-Semitism is treated as a minor flaw to ignore or look beyond when we judge a person's otherwise "good" character, then all who do so will contribute to its contagion.

Sartre, in his classic essay *Anti-Semite and Jew*, eloquently presented the case for using bigotry to define a person's character and not as a footnote to it. This is sometimes difficult to apply, as in the case when the anti-Semite or racist is someone you know or even, otherwise, respect.

Sartre argued that being an anti-Semite is a choice—it is a prism through which people see the world or events colored by the lens of hate or ignorance. Most people with bigoted views can be rebutted effectively—even moved by accurate information. A campaign to shift attitudes or behavior cannot be effective if what you're seeking to change is not clearly defined as a problem.

Keep in mind that no set of actions creates an anti-Semite; nothing any Jew does creates anti-Semitism in the eyes of a nonprejudiced person. A single Jew can be legitimately criticized for reasons of personality, politics, or behavior. But one who refers to all Jews in a negative, genetically culpable way—Jewish bankers, Jewish slumlords, Jewish bloodsuckers—is focusing on the Jewishness, not the character, of the person—and thus engaging in anti-Semitism. Innocent, ignorant, or malicious, it must be confronted straight on—not explained away as a side point.

Proactive education about anti-Semitism aimed at parents and youths—Jewish and non-Jewish—is critical. Good people need to learn how to detect it and to rebut it, even when anti-Semitism falls short of blatant neo-Nazi propaganda. A community willing to tolerate anti-Semitism as a mere excess will find that it is a sickness that will continue to grow.

These points are also important within the Jewish community itself. "Jewish continuity," as important as it is to the future of the Jewish community, will not succeed if younger Jews, in their classrooms, school yards, and campuses, are intimidated by and made vulnerable to anti-Semitic harassment. Clearly, the battle of anti-Semitism really is not about making America a more "comfortable" place for Jews who lack a strong identity. But, if today's young Jews, while enjoying the fruits of Jewish and American progress against anti-Semitism, are unprepared to counter anti-Semitism or decide that a visible Jewish identity is still an obstacle or danger to their future, "Jewish continuity" will not succeed.

Overintellectualizing about the level of contemporary anti-Semitism may be grist for the academic world, but it will never provide the answer to the Jew whose child, colleague, or friend confronts anti-Semitism face to face.

This book is intended to help reduce anti-Semitism by strategically responding to it. It is not a panacea, nor does it pretend to be the single answer to persistent discrimination against Jews. It is a guide. It has, at its roots, a profound belief in the power and responsibility of an individual to make the right kind of difference—to act, to speak, to work with others, to treat people with respect and understanding, and to ensure that no person suffers alone when targetted by any form of bigotry. We hope you will use it.

Leonard P. Zakim
Executive Director
New England Region
Anti-Defamation League

Why Respond?

Anti-Semitism has been called the classic prejudice.[7] In practice, it includes crude slurs, desecrations of synagogues, jokes based on anti-Semitic stereotypes, social exclusion, the rhetoric and ideology of certain hate groups and extremists, government-tolerated or implemented pogroms, and the attempted extermination of Jews in the Nazi Holocaust.

It is important for those who oppose anti-Semitism and who wish to combat it effectively to understand what it is and how it is defined. It is only when one recognizes the affront that steps can be taken to combat it.

There has long been a debate within the Jewish community about the wisdom of "lowering ourselves into the gutter" and engaging in a serious effort to refute the irrational and malicious lies and arguments of individual anti-Semites or anti-Semitic organizations.

Some say such discussions dignify anti-Semitism or lend credibility to the case put forth by anti-Semites. But many, including Sigmund Livingston, the founder of the Anti-Defamation League, argued forcefully for speaking out. In his 1945 book, *Must Men Hate?*, Livingston wrote:

> The worker in the vineyard does not rid the vineyard of weeds by declaring them to be noxious. He takes a hoe and goes out to uproot the poisonous growth. As in military warfare, the best defense is the offense, so in this age-old warfare against reaction we must launch an offensive of truth against every anti-Semitic citadel of forgery, libel, fraud, and bigotry.[8]

The purpose of this book is to underscore the importance of responding to anti-Semitism. Addressing the myths identified herein does not legitimize them. Rather, responding with

1

facts to the sincere but misinformed or with strategic questions to the ill-intentioned bigot help ensure that these myths won't be allowed to stand unanswered.

It is critical to a healthy society to debunk lies and untruths that, if unrebutted, could foster greater anti-Semitism.

Left unanswered, anti-Semitic charges can further influence individuals or communities who are seeking scapegoats or who, for any number of political, religious, economic, or social reasons, already are inclined to blame or distrust Jews.

Students and journalists, educators and attorneys, political leaders, college faculty, police, and members of the clergy—anybody, whether Jewish, Christian, Muslim, or a member of any other faith, who encounters anti-Semitism will be better able to respond with the information this book imparts.

Let us be clear about a basic premise that underlies this effort. By encouraging and empowering you to respond, we are not suggesting that it is possible or even probable for one to reclaim or to redeem the mind of the anti-Semite. Rational debate based on facts, fairness, and decency will rarely influence those motivated by hatred of any kind.

Our target groups are really the undecided, the neutral observer, those whose factual knowledge is easily shaken by confusing arguments, and those who are just plain ignorant. By rebutting the bigot with facts or presenting thoughtful, sharp questions, you can alter the debate so that those listening will stop questioning whether what they hear is true and make them begin to suspect that the information they hear couldn't possibly be true.

The advertising profession understands the need to influence the opinions and attitudes of specific constituencies. In both the production of commercials and the development of political-campaign ads, it seeks to influence those who have not yet firmly decided on Coke vs. Pepsi or on Kennedy vs. Nixon. Of course, you cannot neglect those who have already made their decision and embraced your cause. They require shoring up and support. It is always important to reinforce the views of those who agree with you. Nevertheless, the real audience that commercial and political ads seek to influence is the undecided. That is our audience as well.

Consider the example of the landmark 1960 Presidential debates between Senator John F. Kennedy and Vice-President

"PRETEXTS CHANGE BUT HATRED REMAINS. JEWS ARE NOT HATED BECAUSE THEY ARE EVIL—EVIL QUALITIES ARE SOUGHT IN THEM BECAUSE THEY ARE HATED. IF EVIL QUALITIES DO NOT EXIST, HATRED DEMANDS THAT THEY BE INVENTED."
MAX NORDAU

Richard M. Nixon. According to many political analysts, a critical component of Kennedy's perceived victory was his strategic assessment of whose opinions of him mattered more—those of the American people or Nixon's. Kennedy won the debates by directing his answers to the television audience. By not talking back to Nixon, as in the classic debate form, but instead talking directly to the television audience, Kennedy talked to America. The lesson to be learned is that we need to frame our debates with our detractors in such a way as to influence those in the audience who may be listening. By reaching out to new constituencies who can serve as our allies, we are moving beyond the bigot.

The campaign for truth is both a factual and a strategic one. It begins with you and your own circle of family, friends, and colleagues. It should begin with your own rejection of the anti-Semitic and racist slurs and comments that you may hear.

But suffer no illusions. Entering the debate and challenging those who engage in anti-Semitism will rarely be easy. The circumstances of each encounter will need to be considered in formulating what, if any, response will be both effective and appropriate. Often, the perpetrator will be stunned by your challenge and may simply be ignorant of the fact that using a phrase like "jewed them down" is, in fact, anti-Semitic. The more sophisticated bigot will ridicule your challenge and seek to put you on the defensive, claiming that you are hypersensitive to any comments about Jews, or accusing you of misinterpreting legitimate criticism of Israel as anti-Semitism. You will need to keep your cool and press forward on the merits of your argument.

While overt anti-Semitism—which often expressly reiterates centuries' old canards and stereotypes—is broadly condemned today, newer, more sophisticated, and indirect forms are becoming increasingly more acceptable in some circles, particularly on the college campus. For instance, Holocaust denial, some anti-Semitic theories of Afro-centrism, "JAP-baiting," and the tendency to exclude Jews from multiculturalism have all contributed to a weakened response to anti-Semitism in the college community.

Nowhere is that more clear than in the ongoing campaign of Holocaust denial. In a July 1993 book review printed in the *New York Times*, Walter Reich, then a senior scholar at the Woodrow Wilson Center in Washington, wrote:

The success of Holocaust deniers is also the product of an age in which the freedom to express views is confused with an obligation to facilitate their expression…this success has been the product of an age that promotes the idea that every issue must have two sides, and that each side should be accorded equal respect in the marketplace of discussion. This approach to ideas is fostered by a number of current assumptions, increasingly popular in academia, regarding the indeterminacy of truth, as well as by the modern phenomenon of television talk shows and the journalistic ethos that no news story is complete unless all views about it are aired, including the most absurd and discredited.[9]

As we enter the next century and as the absurd becomes more acceptable, an informed response to anti-Semitism is our responsibility. Let us remember, that over the years, we have in many ways succeeded in keeping anti-Semitic attitudes out of the mainstream of American public opinion. We have made significant progress in reducing anti-Semitic attitudes and barriers, an achievement that should inspire us to believe that change is possible—if we fight for it.

How Do We Respond?

Note to Reader:

The following section provides important strategic guidelines for effectively responding to anti-Semitism. Additionally, points 3–6 provide an array of suggested strategic answers to the charges addressed. You will note that the sample answers proposed reflect the need for a generous mix of facts, strategy, and good judgment.

1. Know Your Facts.

Fight fiction, half-truths, and out-of-context allegations with facts whenever possible. Beware of the use by your opponents of a single anecdotal situation to justify an anti-Semitic position, such as stories regarding the "one" Jewish slave owner, the "one" Jewish racist, and so on. From the traditional charge of Jews seeking economic domination to the Nation of Islam's campaign blaming Jews for the slave trade, facts are the prime tools with which to rebut anti-Semitic propaganda.

At the same time, facts must be used strategically. For example, in addition to drawing on your own knowledge of Holocaust atrocities, quoting Nazi leaders' own admissions about the Final Solution can sometimes be a persuasive response to Holocaust denial. Similarly, instead of relying on moral arguments, it may be more effective to use the Pope's own words about his opposition to anti-Semitism and the untruth of the Christ-killing libel. You must always consider your audience.

2. Know Your Audience.

Each situation requires you to consider the most effective way to respond given who you are, who you are talking to, and the setting you are in. Is it a private incident? Is it public or is it covered by the press? Is the perpetrator a stranger, a public figure, your boss, a customer, client, teacher, clergyperson, Black, Catholic, Arab, Jewish? All of these factors may affect the substance and tone of your response.

If an anti-Semitic statement is made during personal conversation, more often than not you will find the comment to be rooted in ignorance. The comment may reflect the individual's unquestioning acceptance of age-old stereotypes. Embarrassment may be his or her first reaction to you, and your quick response may be immediately effective.

In some cases, however, the response to you will be hostile and very personal. Be prepared. Politeness, fairness, and effectiveness do not require you to debate each issue on the terms set by the bigot or to answer every question the way it is asked. Use each question as an opportunity to present your own information.

If you are in a public forum with speakers like the anti-Semitic Khalid Muhammad, or, former neo-Nazi and Klansman, David Duke, be respectful of the speaker, no matter how much you oppose his or her views, and at the same time, show respect to the crowd. If possible, strategize with allies in advance. Do not monopolize the microphone; it angers people. Keep in mind that this is not a personal battle of egos. It is a battle for opinion that will continue long after the session is over.

Don't try to win the argument or expect someone like skinhead leader Tom Metzger to say, "Hey, you've got me thinking about what you're saying, you're right." In a public forum, your goal is to persuade the people in the crowd or in the classroom that the extremist speaker is a sorry character with no motive other than anti-Semitism and no truth or logic behind his or her rhetoric. You will not accomplish this if you get caught up in a verbal shouting match, expressing ridicule or anger. Your goal is to be heard by the audience—not to convert the speaker.

3. Highlight the Absurdity of a Stereotype.

Anti-Semitic attitudes and stereotypes, such as that "all Jews are dishonest in business," "obsessed with money," "too pushy," etc., are declining, but they continue to be reflected in buzzwords and are reinforced in literature, rap music, and movies. Such remarks don't require a factual response so much as a strategic one. Using humor, sarcasm, or intellectual reasoning, ask your opponent to consider his or her own motives. Be prepared with brief but incisive analogies that deflate the myths and stereotypes. For example, if responding to anti-Semitic comments such as:

• "All Jews are cheap"—You might respond by asking your opponents: Are all Blacks lazy or good athletes? Are all Italians Mafia-members or romantics? Are all men insensitive louts? Are all women weak and emotional?

• "Jewish landlords exploit their tenants"—In response, you might ask whether the speaker knows anything about the performance record of Irish and other landlords—or didn't he or she even bother comparing what rents they charge or the condition of their units?

• "Jewish store owners charge too much interest on loans"—In response, you might question the speaker as to how the percentage charged compared with what the "Yankee" drugstore owner charged. And add: "Oh, you never bothered to look into that; why not?"

• "The Jewish union-organizers were too aggressive"—In response, you should ask your opponent how he or she would describe the approaches of the Irish, Italian, Black, or Polish union-organizers. Aren't union-organizers aggressive by definition? *This is the main point:* What does the religion, color, or ethnic background of the criticized individual have to do with his or her offense? Using this premise, any person who alleges that "all" members of a given group behave alike can be swiftly exposed for his or her bigotry.

4. Concede Negative Truths.

Yes, you can concede serious mistakes or historical events that do not reflect well on Jews. Jews do not need a record of perfection to make anti-Semitism intolerable. Concede such a point early on to better control the agenda and to cut through the need for a defensive posture. Certainly, do not deny what is easily proven, lest you lose credibility. Try and do this while calling into question your opponent's views. For example:

• On the subject of Israel's trade with South Africa— Acknowledge that yes, Israel did trade with South Africa's apartheid regime. And although Israel's trade with South Africa was less than half of one percent of its total trade and was dwarfed by South Africa's trade relationships with Black Africa, Japan, the United States, and Saudi Arabia, Israel is still legitimately included among the nations criticized. However, in light of these facts you should ask why, for years, Israel was the country whose role was most singled out for criticism, as if apartheid stayed alive solely because of Jewish support.

• On the allegation that there are too many Jews in cer- tain professions, such as the law—Point out that many people believe that this country has too many lawyers, period. Challenge your opponent to explain why he or she is focusing solely on Jewish lawyers. Ask the crucial questions: What about Catholic and Protestant lawyers? Shouldn't people of all backgrounds have the right to pursue the professions of their choice as individuals, not as representatives of their eth- nic or religious groups?

5. Don't Demean Anyone Else's Pain.

Any attempt to blame Jews for causing anti-Semitism must be rejected just as any other "blame the victim" approach should be. In the process of articulating a quick and effective response against anti-Semitic charges, one should include an expression of anger, sympathy, or rejection of all forms of bigotry. This is particularly important when con- fronted with individuals who seek to diminish the problems of anti-Semitism by comparing it to other "isms" (racism, sex- ism, homophobia, etc.) which they argue are more serious. Avoid the futile exercise of comparing pain; acknowledge it. Acknowledging one form of oppression does not negate the existence of any other, including anti-Semitism.

It is also essential to apply this strategy whenever someone who claims to reject racist or sexist stereotypes defends or uti- lizes anti-Semitism in the process. We should acknowledge the problems of racism *and* argue against anti-Semitism. For example, one response could be: "I too deplore racism in this country, its roots in slavery, its tragic impact on us all as peo- ple, and the injustices it perpetuates. The tolerance many White people seem to show for racism is appalling. It is

America's greatest shame. However, it defies logic to employ anti-Semitism as a vehicle for denouncing racism."

6. Appeal to a Sense of Fairness and Decency.

Remember it is the audience you are seeking to influence—not the bigot. Avoid name calling and countercharges. Stay above the fray as much as possible by respecting the concerns of your audience. For example:

• When speaking with a representative of a religious group, you might say, "As one who has great respect for religious leaders, I am really astonished by your use of blatant hate. The prophet Malachi (2:10) asked, 'Have we not all one father, has not one God created us?' Isn't this not a central theological theme for all of us?"

• When attempting to refute the sometimes alleged Israel-Nazi equation you might say, "I particularly cannot accept an analogy between the Nazis and Israelis. The official Nazi policy was to exterminate all Jews. They succeeded in killing two-thirds of the Jews in Europe—six million people, including 1.25 million children. Israel, like other nations, is far from perfect. However, it does not have as either an implied or explicit policy the rounding up of Palestinians for the purpose of genocide. Nor has Israel's democracy excluded Palestinians from its protection."

Further, point out that the attempt to analogize Israelis with Nazis is clearly an attempt to hurt Jews in light of the painful history of the Holocaust.

7. Recognize "Polite" Anti-Semitism.

Few manifestations of anti-Semitism are as difficult to handle as those which can be characterized as examples of "polite" anti-Semitism. Although rooted in the same centuries-old anti-Semitic stereotypes that extremists and demagogues typically exploit, polite anti-Semitism rarely, if ever, is expressed through overtly hostile acts.

Instead, it can range from bigoted and ignorant remarks to subtle innuendo by otherwise intelligent and sensible people. Some might refer to Jews as "too pushy" or use the phrase "jewed him down." Others might simply expect their Jewish friends or colleagues to "be good with money" or "well-connected to people of influence." Some might pass comments, such as "they complain too much about the Holocaust" or "all they care about is doing their nails and shopping." As with the other forms of anti-Semitism, one must be careful not to confuse legitimate criticism of individual Jews with generalized allegations about so-called "Jewish" conduct which constitute anti-Semitism.

Like all stereotypes, anti-Semitic stereotypes can be responded to by questioning the generalizations stated.

Remarks like "Jews need to dominate everything," or "you can't trust a Jew" can effectively be interrupted simply by saying, "What do you mean by that?" A simple, rational question politely, but firmly posed can provoke substantial embarrassment to the speaker. Other illogical and unproved generalizations, such as "bad women drivers," "all Italians belong to the Mafia," and "all Irish drink too much," can be interrupted in the same way. In fact, it is the interruption—the unexpected challenge—that makes the difference.

Where a more substantial discussion involving facts and history is called for, you can explain the origins of such stereotypical comments as those above. This is quite helpful, as stereotypes often keep people from getting to know individuals belonging to the groups stereotyped. To assume that Sandy is rich because she is Jewish or that Mike is a great basketball player because he is Black denies their individuality—and often will be plain wrong.

How have such faulty ideas permeated society? Robert Wistrich, author of *ANTISEMITISM: The Longest Hatred*, explains:

> This hostile collective stereotype of a Jewish people bearing the mark of Cain, a nation of Christ-killers, and infidels in league with the Devil, became deeply embedded in the Western psyche following the massacres of Jews during the Crusades.... As Christianity spread among all the peoples of Europe, this devastating image crystallized until it was an integral part of European and Western culture, a fact which, more than any other, accounts for the pervasiveness of anti-Semitism to this day.[10]

Thus, one may be taken aback when a prominent businessman expresses surprise that a Jewish woman enjoys camping, or when an Italian girl is assaulted with anti-Semitic slurs because she is carrying a Bloomingdale's bag, or when a multicultural training facilitator is ignorant of the fact that there are poor Jews. In light of the above-detailed historical reality, one should not be shocked at all.

Do not ignore expressions of anti-Semitism no matter how subtle or because of a notion that they are trivial or insignificant. The person who makes a thoughtless remark today may be more hostile the next time. The person who is hostile to Jews and to others must be confronted. Pushing people to justify their stereotypes with facts can produce an immediate concession of ignorance—or, at least, plant seeds for thought.

Below are some common situations that may arise with suggestions for dealing with them:

• A coworker complains that all Jews are rich—or that all Jews are cheap—or states that he or she "jewed someone down." Respond by telling your coworker that you are offended by this insensitive stereotype. Challenge the person to consider the source of such comments or attitudes. Explore whether they are based on experience or hearsay.

• A friend tells "Jewish-American Princess" ("JAP") jokes. Ask this person whether he or she really understands the expression. Explain that such jokes are offensive, and that they perpetuate degrading stereotypes of Jews and women. Point out that violent anti-Jewish behavior has been associated with this form of verbal abuse, as it is facilitated by its social acceptability.

Let's be clear. Stereotypes are rooted in prejudice. They are not simply indiscretions to be tolerated. They contribute to the dehumanization of an individual. They directly affect the way an individual is greeted and treated by others. They promote erroneous assumptions about a person's work habits, intelligence, cultural habits, tastes in food, sports or mechanical abilities, political views, and ambitions. Relying on such erroneous assumptions is more than a social flaw. It is a political, business, and interpersonal mistake in judgment that should not be tolerated.

"THE LESSON WE MUST LEARN FROM THIS (THE HOLOCAUST) IS THAT EVERYONE OF US CAN AND MUST REACT TO EVERYDAY EXCLUSION AND DISCRIMINATION. MOST WRONGS BEGIN ON A SCALE WHERE THEY CAN STILL BE COMBATTED WITH SPIRIT AND THE COURAGE OF ONE'S CONVICTIONS."

ROMAN HERZOG PRESIDENT, FEDERAL REPUBLIC OF GERMANY

Anti-Semitic Myths

Note to the Reader:

This chapter explores anti-Semitic myths that continue to find currency in both public and private discourse today. Each section contains a brief historical background exploring the origin of the specific myth followed by contemporary examples and suggestions for response. The myths are presented as they arose chronologically, following the development of anti-Semitism through history—starting in its early religious roots and continuing through its broad racial, political, and current-day manifestations. We urge interested readers to consult the bibliography for books providing additional information on the historical origins of the myths.

"They killed Jesus"

Background:

The belief that "the Jews" killed Jesus arose from interpretations of the trial and crucifixion sequences in the four Gospels of the New Testament. The Gospels describe Jewish religious leaders, supported by many followers, delivering Jesus to the Roman authorities, with the request that he be executed as a blasphemer and public menace (the details of the account differ in each of the Gospels).

This charge of deicide has "provided the cornerstone of Christian anti-Semitism"[11] and for centuries Jews have suffered at the hands of Christians because they are believed to have been the murderers of Christ. In ninth-century Spain, Jews received a blow on the face each year on Good Friday in retribution for the crucifixion.[12] The Crusades of the eleventh through thirteenth centuries, in which Jews were either forced to convert or tortured or killed, embedded "the notion of Christ-killers more firmly in the mass consciousness."[13] During the Second Crusade, it was recorded that a Jew was stabbed in five places "in memory of the wounds suffered by Jesus."[14] The myth of Jews committing ritual murder, which emerged in the Middle Ages, was explained as a Jewish penchant for reenacting the crucifixion. In 1890, Alexander III of Russia refused to ease the oppression of Jews in his empire, noting: "But we must not forget that the Jews crucified Christ."[15]

In 1965, the Second Vatican Council issued *Nostra Aetate*, a declaration which stated that the charge of deicide "cannot be charged against all Jews, without distinction, then alive, or against the Jews of today."[16] Various clarifications and elaborations of *Nostra Aetate* have since been released.

Contemporary Examples:

• In the late 1980s, an anti-Semitic book, entitled *The Score*, by Rudy "Butch" Stanko, opened with the following epigraph: "This book is dedicated to Jesus Christ. He was the first to tell the score about the conspiracy of the Sanhedrin and its followers. For this they crucified him."[17] The author wrote the book while in prison and was considered for the position of Pontifex Maximus in the Church of the Creator, an anti-Semitic and racist organization.

• In a speech delivered in Baltimore, in 1994, Khalid Muhammad, then National Spokesman for the Nation of Islam, a racist and extremist organization said, "It was the so-called Jews that set up a kangaroo court to charge Jesus with heresy, and accepted a thief and a robber named Barrabas over the good Black man Jesus, and under a system of capital punishment ordered the death penalty for Jesus, the Black revolutionary Messiah."[18]

• A 1992 study of Protestant Sunday school texts revealed that until that year the United Methodist Church, which used a text ranked most positive in its presentation of Jews, continued "to include statements that the Jews are to blame for the crucifixion of Jesus."[19]

• The script for the production of the Oberammergau Passion Play to be performed in the Bavarian town of Oberammergau, Germany from May 22–September 29, 2000 invokes the deicide charge. According to ADL's Director of Interfaith Affairs, Rabbi Leon Klenicki who analyzed the script, the millennium production "portrays very negative images of Jews and Judaism in the first century, accusing Jewish leadership for Jesus' death and portraying Judaism as void of meaning and spiritually decadent."[20] The Oberammergau play dates back to 1633, when the region was ravaged by the Black Plague. At that time, local townspeople vowed to stage a Passion Play commemorating the story of Jesus' death every ten years.

Responses:

• In *Jesus: A Life*, A. N. Wilson reviews the inconsistencies in the Gospels to dispel the myth that the Jews were responsible for Jesus' death:

> The only hard historical fact we possess is that Jesus was crucified: that is to say, he was condemned by the Romans, and this is a fact which the early Christian church, themselves fearful of persecution did their best to obscure. They therefore blamed the death of Jesus on the Jews, invented the idea that Jesus had been condemned by the Jews for blasphemy, or for plotting to destroy the Temple.[21]

Wilson presents a more likely scenario. Jesus, a committed Jew and prophet, had a following and had created a stir in the Temple. In a crowded city like Jerusalem, the Romans were always concerned about an uprising. The Jewish religious authorities were equally concerned, as they were usually the ones made to suffer for any insurrection. The Jewish authorities may have had to identify the individual Jesus to the Roman authorities as a way of saving the larger community.

• In 1992, the Catechism of the Catholic Church (CCC) was officially released. The document serves as a guide to teaching within the Catholic church. Citing paragraph (597), entitled "The Jews are Not Collectively Responsible for the Death of Jesus," Dr. Eugene Fisher of the National Conference of Catholic Bishops writes:

> Emphasizing 'the historical complexity of Jesus' trial' as "apparent in the Gospels," (597) [the document] notes that even the "personal guilt of those involved (Judas, the Sanhedrin, Pilate) is known only to God alone.' How much less then, the Catechism concludes, 'can we attribute the responsibility for its outcome to all the Jews of Jerusalem?... Still less,' it concludes, 'can we extend the responsibility to other Jews of different places and times.'[22]

• In his own review of the death of Jesus of Nazareth, Dr. Eugene Fisher offers several clarifications which dispel the myth of Jewish guilt:

> Crucifixion, was a Roman form of punishment.... In Jewish law the punishment for blasphemy was death by stoning at the hands of 'all Israel....' If Jesus had been convicted of blasphemy by a formal Jewish court... crucifixion by a third party would not have satisfied the requirements of the law.... Nor is there anything in Jesus' teaching that would constitute "blasphemy" in a legal sense under Jewish law.[23]

• In another article, Dr. Fisher observes that:

> The night arrest of Jesus and the secrecy with which He was questioned illustrate the strong support Jesus enjoyed. Far from wishing His death, the people of Jerusalem mourned His execution by Roman hands (Luke 23:27).[23a]

As far back as pagan times, Jews—a separatist, monotheistic minority in a pagan world—were accused of horrible deeds. The pagan historian Apion maintained that it was Jewish practice to kill and eat their enemies, an absurdity refuted by the Jewish historian Josephus Flavius.[24]

"They poison our wells"

Background:

Several versions of this charge have cropped up in different guises in the centuries after Jesus' death—as an emerging Christian theology rendered Jews God's forsaken people.

From 1347 to 1350, during the spread of the bubonic plague, the Jews were accused of causing the Black Death by poisoning wells. As early as 1144, they were accused in England of ritual murder—killing Christian children in order to use their blood for baking matzos. The "blood libel," as it is called, has been particularly durable. In 1255, when it was again leveled against Jews in Lincoln, England, eighteen Jews were hanged without trial. The event was immortalized by Chaucer in *The Prioress's Tale*, and in many folk songs, twenty-one of which are collected in F. J. Child's *English and Scottish Popular Ballads*.[25] Similar charges have been made in every century throughout Europe.

Following the Damascus blood libel of 1840, nine Jewish leaders were arrested and tortured; two died in prison and seven others were condemned to death.[26] In this century, in Czarist Russia, in 1911, Menahem Mendel Beilis was accused of having murdered a young boy. Despite an investigation establishing that the boy had been killed by non-Jews, the government declared that Beilis had committed the crime because the boy's blood was needed for baking matzos for Passover.[26a] In the United States, at least four cases of blood libel have been documented from the early part of this century. Cases in New York, Massachusetts, Illinois and Minnesota all cited the disappearance of a Christian child. Each case led to public allegations that local Jews had murdered the child for ritualistic purposes.[26b]

Contemporary Examples:

• In 1988, Steve Cokely, an aide to Chicago mayor Eugene Sawyer, charged Jewish doctors with injecting Blacks with the AIDS virus. In the wake of this charge, a faction of the Chicago Black Hebrews alleged that the AIDS virus was deliberately created by Israel and South Africa as a weapon against Blacks. The charge was repeated by Professor Griff, then the "Minister of Information" of the popular rap group Public Enemy. As was reported in a *New York Newsday* editorial: "In an interview with the *Washington Times*, Griff argued that Jews financed these experiments on AIDS with Black people in South Africa."[27]

• In 1991, it was reported that Nabila Shaalan, a Syrian delegate to the UN Human Rights Commission, suggested in an address from the floor that fellow commissioners read the 1983 book, *The Matzoh of Zion*, prefaced by the Syrian defense minister Major Mustafa Tlass, which asserts as fact the 1840 blood libel against Jews in Damascus. The libel was repudiated at the time by the sultanate of Turkey, which then ruled Syria. But Shaalan said that this is a "valuable book" that confirmed and unmasked the racist character of Zionism.[28]

• The *Los Angeles Times* reported, in 1992, that the Egyptian government arrested a family of Israeli Arabs in Egypt on suspicion that they were agents of the Mossad, the Israeli intelligence agency. Articles in the Egyptian press claimed that the daughter, seventeen-year-old Faika, was an AIDS carrier and had been sent to infect young Egyptian males.[29]

• In a nationally publicized speech, in November 1993, at New Jersey's Kean College, then Nation of Islam National Spokesman, Khalid Abdul Muhammad said, "Who is it sucking our blood in the Black community?... They sell us pork, and they don't even eat it themselves. A meat case full of rotten pork meat and the impostor Arab and the impostor White Jew, neither of them eat it themselves."[30]

• In April 1998, a man was arrested in Miami Beach, Florida for picketing the Holocaust Memorial bearing a large placard accusing Jews of committing ritual murders of Christian children.[30a]

• A May 1999 article in the government-controlled *El Wattan* newspaper in Oman, invoked the blood libel charge. The article, titled "Matzas of Blood," reported that during the Jewish holiday of Passover, Jews eat matza "baked with human blood, Christian blood in particular."[30b]

Responses:

• One response to the origins of the charge is offered by Professor Gavin Langmuir of Stanford University, and may well apply to modern manifestations:

These projections of ritual murder, host desecration, and well-poisoning inevitably assumed a religious coloration, but, in fact, they owe more to tensions within the majority society and the psychological problems of individuals than to the real conflict between Christianity and Judaism.... They imagined 'Jews' according to their threatened beliefs.[31]

• Those who propose that Jews spread the AIDS virus will, of course, be unable to cite a single piece of evidence supporting their claim. In some circumstances, it may also be helpful to point out that, in fact, many doctors who are Jewish have been at the forefront of research to combat AIDS and other diseases. For instance, Salk and Sabin worked on the polio vaccine, and, at the time of his death, Salk was working on a vaccine for AIDS. Dr. Matilda Krim is a Jewish doctor who codirects the American Foundation for AIDS Research. Béla Schick discovered the test for diphtheria, and Dr. Selman Waksman discovered streptomycin for the treatment of tuberculosis.

• The absurdity of the charge of ritual murder for the purposes of using Christian blood for the baking of matzos is underscored by Jewish dietary laws, which specifically forbid the consumption of blood. Additionally, rules are prescribed for soaking and salting meat in order to remove blood—a primary condition for kosher meat to this day. According to the Hebrew Bible (Deut. 12:23–25), Jews are instructed:

> Only be sure that thou eat not the blood; for the blood is the life; and thou mayst not eat the life with the meat. Thou shalt not eat it; thou shalt pour it out upon the earth like water. Thou shalt not eat it; that it may go well with thee, and with thy children after thee, when thou shalt do that which is right in the sight of the Lord.[32]

"They control the money"

Background:

The stereotype of the Jew as the embodiment of greed dates to medieval times. In the medieval world, Jews had been forced into the role of moneylenders. This was partly because they were forbidden to own land and to join many of the craft guilds, and partly because the Church had forbidden Christians from lending money at interest. Usury was condemned as a sin against nature and society. But, since Jews were not subject to Christian law and Jewish law prohibited usury only among fellow Jews, not non-Jews, and kings and nobles needed cash to run their fiefdoms, both the Church and the state appointed Jews as moneylenders and tax-collectors.

Unsurprisingly, the notion that Jews aspired to world financial domination gained broader currency with the rise in the nineteenth century of conspiracy theories alleging a Jewish plot to rule the world. Two corollaries of the financial-control myth proved especially durable in the United States in the twentieth century: Jews control the banking industry and the Federal Reserve bank system.

Contemporary Examples:

• In January 1987, it was widely reported in the American press that a Japanese newspaper, *Yomiuri Shinbun*, published an article, entitled "Last-Ditch Fight to Save the Yen: The Jewish Capital Conspiracy Theory." The article stated, "At the Bank of Japan, troubled by the high yen, a certain book has quietly become a best seller.... It explains that 'the high yen is the result of a plot to beat the black-ink country Japan down by international Jewish capital, which holds the crucial levers of power in America.'"[33] The author of the book, *When You Understand the Jews, You Begin to Understand the World*, was identified as Uno Masami, a longtime anti-Semitic propagandist and conspiracy-monger.

• Mainstream publications and politicians have sometimes appeared insensitive to anti-Semitic imagery. In 1991, a scandal at the Wall Street firm of Salomon Brothers was prominently featured in a widely read New England daily. In describing the CEO's role in the rise of the firm to a position of influence on Wall Street, the *Boston Globe* wrote that his reputation as a "super-aggressive bidder for corporate bond issues" and "his instincts for the market, and his guts in bidding for outsized portions of securities helped Salomon make the transition from small Jewish bond house to major global investment banker."[34]

• In 1991, Pat Robertson, founder of the Christian Coalition, authored the book *The New World Order*. In it, he repeatedly uses the term "European bankers" (a common euphemism among extremists to denote a Jewish conspiracy to control world finance) to illustrate what he sees as a world-wide conspiracy of financiers and politicians, many with Jewish names. Robertson explains that the conspirators gained control of all of the sources of world finance through the Rothschild banking empire, a well-known, Jewish-owned entity.[35]

• In April of 1992, *New York Newsday* and the *New York Times* reported that at a Wall Street rally, former California Governor Jerry Brown spoke of "driving the moneylenders from the temple, and reciting a list that included Jewish-sounding names from a *Business Week* article about Clinton's Wall Street supporters."[36]

• In a nationally publicized speech given at Kean College in New Jersey, in November 1993, Khalid Abdul Muhammad, then Nation of Islam National Spokesman, said, "We found out then that the Federal Reserve ain't really owned by the Federal government, the Federal Reserve is owned by.... It's owned by Jews."[37]

Responses:

• While it is true that some Jews are among the most affluent citizens in the United States, there appears to be an exclusive association of Jews with the negative characteristics of power, corruption, greed, and manipulation. This stereotype assumes that when Jews strive for success and prosperity, goals all Americans are encouraged and entitled to pursue, they act illegitimately and conspiratorially. The absurd notion that two to three percent of the population could control everyone else's money rests on this sort of demonization. In fact, the traditions that Jews, like members of other ethnic groups, bring to our society benefit and enrich American culture overall.

• Indeed, stereotypes attributed to Jews are not directed to other groups whose economic wealth is disproportionate to their numbers. For example, most banks in the United States are owned by Protestants; Jews have traditionally made up a minute percentage of the top officers and board members of

American commercial banks and even less of savings banks.[38] Yet, these facts have not put an end to the allegation that Jews control the banks. Neither has the reality that members of other groups are equally affluent, nor that a portion of the Jewish population lives in poverty, retired the notion that Jews have a predisposition to make and handle money. In fact, by relying on statistics to disprove Jewish "control," we must be careful of unwittingly playing the anti-Semite's game. The illogical and prejudiced notion that Jews in any field act in concert with other Jews similarly situated simply because they happen to be Jews, should be rejected.

• The Federal Reserve bank system is the nation's central bank, charged with administering and making policy on American credit and monetary affairs. The Federal Reserve is overseen by a seven-member Board of Governors. Each member is appointed by the President of the United States and confirmed by the United States Senate. Economists of Jewish and non-Jewish backgrounds alike have advocated higher taxes and other financial measures deemed to be in the national interest. For example, despite their service in different Republican and Democratic administrations, fiscal conservative Paul Volcker, who served in the early 1980s as head of the Federal Reserve Board, and the Board's current chair, Alan Greenspan, share a similar economic philosophy. Greenspan is Jewish; Volcker is not. Yet, they have raised and lowered interest rates based on their shared ideology, not on their religions.

"They're cheap"

Background:

The England of Shakespeare had few Jews when he wrote *The Merchant of Venice*, since they had been expelled in the thirteenth century. Yet, when he created the inhumane, greedy character of Shylock, Shakespeare drew from an easily recognizable stereotype which was already centuries old. Christian teachings concerning the accursedness of the Jews radiated out into all aspects of English culture. Once the Church had created a socially accepted scapegoat, the dramatist and the writer had a ready made villain to exploit in their works. The hook-nosed, red-bearded Judas evolved in

Two books that have helped shape anti-Semitic attitudes.

Elizabethan drama into the characters of Barrabas and Shylock. Their very features were enough to remind the audience of the connection that existed between these men and the Jew who betrayed Jesus for thirty pieces of silver.[39]

In 1838, Charles Dickens drew on that same stereotype for the character Fagin, in his book *Oliver Twist*; no wonder the two characters are strikingly similar, despite the 250 years between their appearances.

Contemporary Examples:

• In 1985, after viewing a video about landlord/tenant relations, in which the *tenant* was clearly identified as being Jewish, seventy percent of the viewing audience asserted that the stingy *landlord* was the Jew.

• In the late 1980s, the senior physician at an American medical foundation commented to a Jewish colleague that some patients from abroad attempted to "jew [him] down when the bill was presented for services." When the colleague objected to the use of the term, the physician sent him a letter saying: "The Bible describes Jews as 'a stiff-necked people' (Exod. 32:9), but you carry the trait to self-destructive extremes."[40]

• In June of 1991, a prosecuting attorney, in his summation to a jury, repeatedly made oblique references to Shakespeare's *The Merchant of Venice*. "Repeatedly referencing the Shylock character, the prosecutor spoke of the defendant's alleged greed and deceit, conjuring the image for the jury of the age-old anti-Semitic stereotype."[41]

• In December 1998 on a college campus in New Jersey, one student yelled to another, "You're a stereotypical lazy Jew and all you care about is your money."[41a]

Responses:

• The assumption that the actions of a few typify the behavior of all is at the heart of bigotry. Every ethnic or religious group, Jews included, numbers individuals who are cheap or stingy with their money. It is a *human* characteristic. The charge that Jews are innately miserly (or that miserliness is innately Jewish) engages grotesque medieval stereotypes of the despised, accursed Jew.

• If you had tough negotiations with an Italian grocery store owner or lawyer, would you think all Italians were obsessed with money? If you discovered that a Korean store owner overcharged you, would you suspect all Korean store owners of being cheap? If the Italian store owner was honest and fair with you, would you note that he was an honest Italian merchant—or just honest? If he was Jewish, would he be an honest store owner—for a Jew?

• Jewish communal structures are designed to take care of their own community financially and otherwise, but, like other Americans, Jews recognize their stake and responsibility for improving the welfare of the country as a whole. The tradition of American Jewish philanthropy is a defining characteristic of American Jewish culture, yet, citing it to counter specific charges of Jewish cheapness may often be inappropriate. One need not prove Jewish generosity. Nevertheless, the record of Jewish philanthropy is clear: According to a National Jewish Population Survey published in the *American Jewish Yearbook*, 80.25% of Jews give to Jewish causes, while 70.75% of Jews give to secular charities.[42]

"They conspire to control the world"

Background:

With the emergence of pseudoscientific racial theories in the nineteenth century, "Jewishness" increasingly was seen as biologically determined. Anti-Jewish rhetoric became racialized, as did the idea of nationhood. Jews were excluded from these racist definitions of nationality, and came to be seen as an "external" threat to the nations in which they lived. Conspiracy theories proliferated.

In France, in 1870, Henri Gougenot des Mousseaux published a book in which he denounced the "Judaization of the Christian people" through the secret forces of Freemasonry and liberal rationalism. According to his argument, international Jewry (directed from Paris by the Alliance Israélite Universelle) aimed to rule the world by promoting liberalism and secularism against Christianity. In 1886, Edouard-Adolphe Drumont published a best seller called *La France Juive* (*Jewish France*), whose central theme was that the Jews had seized power in France since the Revolution of 1789 and were subverting French traditions and culture. Drumont argued that Jews controlled the financial system and were expropriating the masses of French workers.[43]

Around the turn of the century, Russia's Czarist secret police (*Okhrana*) wrote the *Protocols of the Learned Elders of Zion*, which purported to be details of a plan by Jewish leaders to attain world domination. The Okhrana claimed to have stolen the *Protocols* from the (nonexistent) Zionist headquarters in France. In 1917, the Czarists portrayed the Bolshevik revolution as part of a Jewish plot to enslave the world, pointing to the *Protocols* as the blueprint. In the 1920s, two British correspondents who had lived in pre-Revolutionary Russia promoted the idea of a Jewish conspiracy in Great Britain and translated the *Protocols* into English, publishing it in the *Morning Post*. In 1921, the Arabs of Palestine and Syria used the *Protocols* to stir up resentment against Jewish settlers in Palestine.[44]

Between May and September of 1920, Henry Ford's *Dearborn Independent* published an American version of the *Protocols* in the series "The International Jew: The World's Foremost Problem." ("The International Jew" also popularized such anti-Semitic myths as Jewish control of industry and the media.) The *Protocols* served to rationalize anti-Semitism and genocide in Hitler's Germany. In our time, the *Protocols* has been translated and circulated in Japan, Latin America, and the Arab world. In 1980, Hazem Nuseibeh, the Jordanian delegate to the UN, spoke about the *Protocols* as if it were a legitimate document. In October 1987, the Iranian Embassy in Brazil circulated copies of the *Protocols*, which it said "belongs to the history of the world."[45]

Contemporary Examples:

• In the early 1970s, copies of the *Protocols of the Learned Elders of Zion* were displayed for sale at the Nation of Islam's main New York City mosque in Harlem. Also in the early 1970s, *Muhammad Speaks*, the weekly publication of the Nation of Islam, carried articles with headlines such as "Vatican-Zionist-racist conspiracy against Africa."[46]

• The 1988 "Principles of Faith" set forth by Hamas, an Islamic fundamentalist group, states, "The Jews control the media and the world financial institutions.... By their evil corruption they try to gain domination of the world by such institutions as the United Nations and its Security Council. More details of their iniquity can be found in the *Protocols of the Learned Elders of Zion*."[47]

• A 1992 hate letter mailed to a prominent Jewish lawyer read:

> It will be our pleasure to hang you and all the scum like you when we crack the (ZOG) Zionist Occupation Government and the Zionist-Masonic Conspiracy that has our country in mental, as well as physical, chains. We will break those chains and drive you bastards out of our country, or hang you or both. Buchanan for President, America First, Death to Zionism.[48]

• In 1992, the *National Vanguard*, a national right-wing extremist publication, stated:

> To make way for themselves to open up possibilities for penetration and control they [Jews] must break down the structure of the society, corrupt its institutions, undermine its solidarity... obliterate its traditions, destroy its homogeneity.[49]

• In a nationally broadcast television interview in April 1997, Louis Farrakahn, head of the Nation of Islam said, "I believe that for the small numbers of Jewish people in the United States, they exercise a tremendous amount of influence on the affairs of government...Yes, they exercise extradordinary control, and Black people will never be free in this country until they are free of that kind of control."[49a]

Responses:

• The charge that Jews plan the destruction of nations and the takeover of the world is especially preposterous when one looks at the long history of persecution of Jews in almost every country they have inhabited.

• For the past sixty years, a wide array of authorities have publicly attested to the fraudulence of the *Protocols:*

1936: Hugo Valentin, professor at the University of Uppsala in Sweden, called the document "the greatest forgery of the century."

1938: Father Pierre Charles, professor at the Jesuit College in Louvain, Belgium, said, "It has been proved that these *Protocols* are a fraud, a clumsy plagiarism... made for the purpose of rendering the Jews odious."

1942: Prominent historians Carl Becker (Cornell University), Sydney Fay and William Langer (Harvard University), Allan Nevins and Carlton J. H. Hays (Columbia University) all endorsed the findings of Professor John Shelton Curtiss that the *Protocols* qualify as "rank and pernicious forgeries."

1962: CIA Assistant Director Richard Helms testified at a Senate hearing, "The Russians have a long tradition in the art of forgery. More than sixty years ago the Czarist intelligence service concocted and peddled a confection called the *Protocols of the Elders of Zion.*"[50]

"Their national loyalty can't be trusted"

Background:

Accusations of dual loyalty are rooted in the Jews' historic separateness and in the conditions of Diaspora life, which was characterized by Jews being denied even the most basic rights of citizenship and acceptance. Charges of dual loyalty—a loyalty toward their religious leaders that was thought to supersede their loyalty to the state—arose at least as early as the first century in the Roman-controlled city of Alexandria, at which time a pogrom (violent assault directed against Jews) ensued.[51]

The classic modern example of doubting the loyalty of Jews to the state is the Dreyfus Case. In 1894, the French General Staff accused Captain Alfred Dreyfus of spying for the Germans. This accusation was made on the basis of a list of documents found in the wastepaper basket of the German military attaché. There was nothing to tie Dreyfus to the document, but the General Staff reasoned that no Christian officer could possibly be guilty of such an offense. Five years later, Dreyfus was brought back from Devil's Island, retried, and convicted of "treason in extenuating circumstances" but pardoned. He demanded an investigation and a retrial. In 1906, he was declared innocent.[52]

In the former Soviet Union, Jews were commonly regarded as traitors and enemies of the state. During the seventy-five years of Soviet communist rule, Jews were often singled out for persecution and sent to labor camps in Siberia. In 1952, the Soviet Jewish condition deteriorated as a result of the infamous "Doctors' Plot," when six Jewish and three non-Jewish doctors were accused of conspiring to poison the Soviet leadership under orders from Western intelligence and the American Jewish Joint Distribution Committee. In 1953, the Soviet-Jewish intelligentsia was liquidated under the pretext that a postwar proposal by the Jewish Anti-Fascist Committee to settle Jews in the Crimea was really a plot to create a pro-Western base within the Soviet Union.[53] In light of this history, it is ironic that after the tight reins of central government have been released, anti-Semitic groups in Russia accuse the Jews of being responsible for the dark years of communism and the ills it brought the Soviet people.

Contemporary Examples:

• In an article in the *Nation*, in March of 1986, novelist Gore Vidal wrote, "Jews are Israel's 'fifth columnists' who stay on among us in order to make propaganda and raise money for Israel."[54]

• In 1991, in opposing United States participation in the Gulf War against Saddam Hussein, columnist and television talk-show host, Pat Buchanan contended that "there are only two groups that are beating the drums for war in the Middle East—the Israeli Defense Ministry and its amen corner in the United States."[55]

• In a 1998 poll of American attitudes, 31% of those polled agreed with the statement, "Jews are more loyal to Israel than America."[56]

• In an October 1998 address before the National Press Club in Washington, DC, Nation of Islam leader Louis Farrakhan said, "Every Jewish person that is around the president is a dual citizen of Israel and the United States of America...And sometimes, we have to raise the question, 'Are you more loyal to the state of Israel than you are to the best interests of the United States of America?'"[56a]

Responses:

• It is important to acknowledge that, given the history of persecution and the fact that Israel has had to overcome formidable odds to survive, Jews do, in fact, have a special relationship with the Jewish State. This, coupled with biblical yearnings for Zion, has engendered a strong kinship between American Jews and Israel. It does not, however, undermine or mitigate American Jewry's national loyalty to the United States.

• United States Supreme Court Justice Louis Brandeis, an ardent and active Zionist, answered the charge of dual loyalty:

> Let no American imagine that Zionism is inconsistent with Patriotism. Multiple loyalties are objectionable only if they are inconsistent.... There is no inconsistency between loyalty to America and loyalty to Jewry.[57]

• Other groups with strong bonds to their "home" country do not face the accusations leveled at Jews. For instance, despite active financial and political support for Ireland, few, if any, accuse Irish-Americans of dual loyalty. This holds true even though Irish-Americans are eligible for Irish citizenship even if only one grandparent was born in Ireland.

• In another example, when two Greek-Americans ran for President, no one suggested that, if elected, they might be influenced by the Greek government to change the status quo on Cyprus in favor of Greece. When the Greek-American Vice-President Spiro Agnew resigned rather than remain to be impeached for perjury, no one accused Greek-Americans as a group of being liars. Lebanese-Americans were not collectively held responsible for the taking and holding of American hostages in Lebanon. Yet, Jews continue to be singled out for alleged disloyalty when they champion their ethnic interests.

• The charge that Jews do not fight in wars on behalf of the United States is an old and baseless anti-Semitic slur. Just like any other group of Americans, tens of thousands of Jewish mothers and widows have mourned for their sons and husbands who have died fighting for this country. Responding to Patrick Buchanan's 1991 charge that American Jews are Israel's "amen corner" and the implication that Jews would

Anti-Semitic rally used to reinforce the concept that the Holocaust never happened.

not be the ones participating in the defense of American interests, conservative icon William F. Buckley, Jr., declared, "I find it impossible to defend Pat Buchanan against the charge that what he did and said during the period under examination amounted to anti-Semitism."[58]

"The Holocaust didn't happen"

Background:

Half a century after the Holocaust, anti-Semitic propagandists have established a movement known as Holocaust "revisionism" to deny that six million Jews were exterminated by the Nazis during World War II.

The leading organization in the Holocaust-denial movement is the California-based Institute for Historical Review (IHR). Founded in 1979, this revisionist outfit was the brainchild of anti-Semite Willis A. Carto. Annual IHR meetings are forums for promoting bizarre theories, such as the allegation that gas chambers never existed at Auschwitz, or that President Roosevelt had advance knowledge of the bombing of Pearl Harbor and allowed it to take place unchecked.

Despite their use of blatantly anti-Semitic theories, the revisionists seek the acceptance of academic audiences, and attempt to cloak themselves in the mantle of legitimate research with their publication, the *Journal for Historical Review*.

As historian Deborah Lipstadt of Emory University wrote in her book, *Denying the Holocaust*:

> In order to maintain their facade as a group whose only objective is the pursuit of truth, the deniers have filled their publication with articles that... are designed to demonstrate that theirs is a global effort to attack and revise historical falsehoods.

Therefore, Lipstadt adds:

> Articles on the Civil War, World War I, and Pearl Harbor are included in their journals as a means of illustrating how establishment historians, with ulterior political motives have repeatedly put forward dis-

torted views of history.... They argue that the tactic of distortion by "court historians" for political means reached its zenith in the Holocaust "myth."[59]

Contemporary Examples:

• Lipstadt cites in *Denying the Holocaust*:

In an interview with *Esquire* magazine, in February 1983, the late actor Robert Mitchum, who played leading roles in the television productions of Herman Wouk's World War II sagas, *Winds of War* and *War and Remembrance*, suggested that there was doubt about the Holocaust. Asked about the slaughter of six million Jews, he replied, 'So the Jews say.' The interviewer, incredulous, repeated Mitchum's comment verbatim, 'So the Jews say?' and Mitchum responded, 'I don't know, people dispute that.'[60]

• In 1986, a United States Court of Appeals decision dismissed a case in which Liberty Lobby, the most anti-Semitic organization in the country, sued the *Wall Street Journal*. The decision noted that: "The *Spotlight*, a publication of Liberty Lobby, has given extensive publicity to the fantastic claim that the Holocaust, the extermination of 6,000,000 Jews by Nazi Germany, never occurred."[61]

• In 1988, Fred A. Leuchter, Jr., a self-proclaimed engineer and expert on death machines, wrote *The Leuchter Report: The End of a Myth*. It was promoted as "an engineering report on the alleged execution chambers at Auschwitz, Birkenau, and Majdanek." It concluded that the gas chambers "could not have been, or now be, utilized or seriously considered to function as execution chambers." Upon returning from a trip to Poland, Leuchter stated, "I was appalled to learn that much of what I was taught about twentieth-century history and World War II was a myth, if not a lie."[62]

• Since 1991, Bradley R. Smith, the founder and a director of the Committee for Open Debate on the Holocaust (CODOH), who has been involved in the Holocaust-denial movement for over a decade, sent an advertisement, entitled "THE HOLOCAUST CONTROVERSY: A CASE FOR OPEN DEBATE," to over fifty college newspapers.[63] As of

"THE BISHOPS OF THE HUNGARIAN CATHOLIC CHURCH...COMMEMORATE IN PIETY THE TRAGIC EVENTS OF FIFTY YEARS AGO, WHEN JEWS LIVING IN HUNGARY WERE DRAGGED TO CONCENTRATION CAMPS AND SLAUGHTERED IN COLD BLOOD. WE CONSIDER IT AS THE GREATEST SHAME OF OUR TWENTIETH CENTURY THAT HUNDREDS OF THOUSANDS OF [HUNGARIAN] LIVES WERE EXTINGUISHED MERELY BECAUSE OF THEIR ORIGIN."

HUNGARIAN CATHOLIC BISHOPS AND ECUMENICAL COUNCIL OF CHURCHES

"IN GERMANY THEY CAME FIRST FOR THE COMMUNISTS, AND I DIDN'T SPEAK UP BECAUSE I WASN'T A COMMUNIST. THEN THEY CAME FOR THE JEWS AND I DIDN'T SPEAK UP BECAUSE I WASN'T A JEW. THEN THEY CAME FOR THE TRADE UNIONISTS AND I DIDN'T SPEAK UP BECAUSE I WASN'T A TRADE UNIONIST. THEN THEY CAME FOR THE CATHOLICS AND I DIDN'T SPEAK UP BECAUSE I WAS A PROTESTANT. THEN THEY CAME FOR ME, AND BY THAT TIME, NO ONE WAS LEFT TO SPEAK UP."

PASTOR MARTIN NIEMOELLER

1999 approximately 140 student papers published versions of the ad including such prestigious institutions as MIT, Cornell and Stanford. An excerpt from the ad reads:

> Holocaust historians depend increasingly on "eyewitness" testimonies to support their theories.... History is filled with stories of masses of people claiming to be eyewitnesses to everything from witchcraft to flying saucers.[64]

Responses:

• The Holocaust is one of the most thoroughly documented events in modern history. Despite the efforts of the Nazi German government to conceal its acts of genocide by suppressing information and deliberately destroying numerous documents, vast documentation remains. The testimonies of scores of survivors, such as Primo Levi and Elie Wiesel; the Nuremberg trials and the Eichmann trial, with their thousands of historical documents; documentary film footage taken by the German army; and photographs of the death camps taken by liberating armies provide overwhelming evidence of the atrocities perpetrated by the Nazis.

• The perpetrators of Nazi crimes themselves have attested to the mass murders of millions of Jews. It can be useful to refer to such testimony in responding to Holocaust denial. For example, Heinrich Himmler, head of the SS, charged with the implementation of the Final Solution, said in a speech in a secret meeting on October 8, 1943:

> We had to answer the question: "What about the women and the children?" Here, too, I had made up my mind, find a clear-cut solution. I did not feel that I had the right to exterminate the men—that is to murder them, or have them murdered—and then allow their children to grow into avengers threatening our sons and grandchildren. A fateful decision had to be made: This people had to vanish from the earth... it has been executed.[65]

Rudolph Hess, while awaiting a sentence of life imprisonment in a Polish jail, in 1946, detailed his duty as first commandant of Auschwitz:

The gassing was carried out in the detention cells of Block II. Protected by a gas mask, I watched the killing myself. In the crowded cells death came instantaneously the moment Zyklon B was thrown in. During the spring of 1942, hundreds of vigorous men and women walked all unsuspecting to their death in the gas chamber.[66]

During his 1960 trial in Israel, Adolph Eichmann recalled the January 20, 1942 Wannsee Conference convened by the Nazis to coordinate the implementation of the Final Solution. Eichmann testified:

These gentlemen…were discussing the subject quite bluntly, quite differently from the language that I had to use later in the record. During the conversation they minced no words at all…they spoke about methods of killing, about liquidation, about extermination.[66a]

• In 1985, on the fortieth anniversary of the surrender of Nazi Germany, the President of Germany, Richard von Weizaecker, said:

Who could remain unsuspecting after the burning of the synagogues, the plundering, the stigmatization with the star of David, the deprivation of rights, the ceaseless violation of human dignity? Whoever opened his eyes and ears could not fail to notice that Jews were being deported.[67]

• In the aftermath of the placement of the aforementioned Holocaust-denial ad by Bradley Smith (see **Contemporary Examples**), the *Harvard Crimson* rejected the ad:

To give CODOH a forum so that it could 'promulgate malicious falsehoods' under the guise of open debate constituted an 'abdication' of the paper's editorial responsibility.[68]

• In December 1993, a *Boston Globe* editorial commented on Brandeis University's student-run paper's choice to run the Holocaust denial ad:

Those who deny the existence of the Nazi death camps and defame the victims do so from the pathological and evil depths. For fools like them there is no remedy. It is pathetic, however, that college journalists… would allow themselves to be manipulated by Holocaust revisionists. The advertising departments of most newspapers keep a useful form letter handy for offensive advertising queries. In the case of Holocaust deniers even such a letter is too much of a courtesy.[69]

"They had a major role in the slave trade"

Background:

The allegation that Jews controlled the slave trade has been given new life with the 1991 publication of the Nation of Islam's *The Secret Relationship Between Blacks and Jews*. This book holds Jews responsible for financing the slave trade and the legacy of racism, violence, and discrimination that resulted from it—a classic example of scapegoating. This is not an entirely new effort. It recalls author Robert Wistrich's description of how Jews came to represent the "personification of evil." Its use of the doctrine of collective guilt links the cause of all evil to the real or imagined evils of a few individual Jews. In doing so it borrows from the notion contained in the infamous *Protocols of the Learned Elders of Zion* of an international Jewish conspiracy with a goal of enslaving all Christians.

In the 1970s and 1980s, these malicious allegations appeared in *Western Front* and *Thunderbolt, Inc.* Both were extremist publications widely read by the Klan and other hate groups. The charges, not unlike the allegations put forward by the authors of the *Secret Relationship*, relied on sources like the anti-Semitic four-volume series "The International Jew," originally published by Henry Ford's *Dearborn Independent*. Similar allegations appeared in other hate publications throughout the past several decades. Among the most recent is that of the *White Patriot*, a Klan publication, which, in its March 1998 issue, alleged that "in fact, almost the entire American slave trade was in the hands of Northern Jews.[70]

"BLACK ANTI-SEMITISM HURTS BLACK PEOPLE FIRST AND FOREMOST. IN PART, BECAUSE IT LEADS US TO THE POLITICS OF DISTRACTION, THE POLITICS OF DISTORTION…ANTI-SEMITISM IS NOT GOING TO HELP US IN THE STRUGGLE AGAINST INJUSTICE, POVERTY, AIDS, AND VIOLENCE. SO WHY MAKE EXCUSES FOR IT?"

HENRY LOUIS GATES, JR.

While there was minimal Jewish involvement in the slave trade, the Nation of Islam and its leader, Louis Farrakhan, greatly magnify its level, reflecting an obsession with Jews. As Harvard professor Cornel West, author of *Race Matters*, explains, in a February 1994 *Time* magazine article, the fact that Farrakhan alleges:

> That Jews owned 75% of enslaved Africans in this country at a time when there were about four million Black slaves and 5,000 Jewish slaveholders reveals this obsession. In fact, in 1861, Jews constituted roughly 0.2% of Southerners (20,000 out of nine million) and 0.3% of slaveholders (5,000 out of 1,937,625).[71]

Contemporary Examples:

• In *Blacks and Jews News*, a publication of the Nation of Islam, a headline declares: "Jews Run Slave Trade." This publication announced the 1991 release of a book, entitled *The Secret Relationship Between Blacks and Jews*. Minister Louis Farrakhan, leader of the Nation of Islam, says the book is an attempt to "rearrange a relationship that is not beneficial to us but has been detrimental to us."[72]

• The unnamed author(s) of *The Secret Relationship Between Blacks and Jews* states that:

> The most prominent of the Jewish Pilgrim fathers used kidnapped Black Africans disproportionately more than any other ethnic or religious group.

The book also claims:

> Jews have been conclusively linked to the greatest criminal endeavor ever undertaken against an entire race of people... the Black African Holocaust.[73]

• In his March 1993 newsletter, entitled *Blacks & Jews at Wellesley News*, Wellesley College Professor Anthony Martin, in reference to *The Secret Relationship* (which he used in one of his courses), wrote that:

> The *Secret Relationship Between Blacks and Jews*, using primarily Jewish sources, shows that Jews were fully involved in every aspect of the African slave trade.[74]

Responses:

• One must not defend any participation in the slave trade—Jewish or not. The earlier it is emphatically noted that slavery was and is unjustified and inhuman, the better. We must be prepared to acknowledge that any Jewish involvement in slavery, however minimal, is fair game for legitimate criticism. Nevertheless, if it is only the Jewish role in slavery that is examined, alarms should go off, especially when that alleged involvement is blatantly distorted.

• The *Secret Relationship* reflects blatant anti-Semitism by disproportionately blaming Jews for the slave trade while excusing others who overwhelmingly engaged in its practice. Its failure to delineate the extensive role played by others, including the Africans, Dutch, and Portuguese, raises further questions about the book's intent.

• The book's broad allegation of group culpability is innately racist.

• The *Secret Relationship* has been the subject of harsh criticism, for its methodology and its conclusions, by both African-American and White historians of slavery, who note that Jews constituted a minute proportion (0.3%) of slaveholders and traders.

• A scholar on slavery, Harvard University Professor Orlando Patterson, stated at an ADL-sponsored forum on multicultural education that:

> The Jews were involved in the slave trade.... The question is what one makes of this fact and how one interprets it. And why are the Jews being singled out? The truth of the matter is that all major Western European powers and many of the minor ones were involved in the slave trade.

> If one says that Jews were disproportionately involved, given their size, one could say the same of the Portuguese, Swedes, or Danes.... I think it's important that in responding to this, one not only get the facts straight but... that we not overreact or suggest that there is no involvement whatever.... I think that what we have to do is simply place it in context, point out that all other groups in Europe were involved, all

of the White people were involved. Point out also, unfortunately, that on the West Coast of Africa there were Black magnates who were very much involved with the selling of their own people to the New World.[75]

In a refutation of the slave trade charge, Professor of History, Saul Friedman writes:

Control of the slave trade, like all commercial activity, was dictated by the rulers of European nation-states. To have influence in any aspect of trade, merchants and bankers had to be close to the crown or a joint stock company. Jews who were banished from one European land to another after the era of the Crusades simply did not enjoy such prominence.[76]

Friedman also notes:

For a people that supposedly masterminded the slave trade, the Jews are remarkably absent from major texts on the subject.[77]

David Brion Davis, Sterling Professor of History at Yale University, underscores this point:

Jews and Jewish names are virtually absent from the texts and indices of all scholarly works on the Atlantic slave trade and from recent monographs on the British, French, Dutch, and Portuguese branches of the commerce in slaves. To expose the supposedly "secret relationship" between Jews and slavery, anti-Semites have therefore turned to histories of the Jews in such regions as Amsterdam, Brazil, and Curaçao. These works provide material that can easily be mis-quoted, distorted, and put in totally misleading con-texts.[78]

• Henry Louis Gates, Jr., Chairman of the African-American Studies Department at Harvard University, writes of the book, *The Secret Relationship Between Blacks and Jews,* that the text:

... is an invidious document of anti-Semitism; that is, it's hard to think of any historical motivation for it other than the fomenting of hostility toward Jews and as a defense for anti-Semitic rhetoric. Unfortunately, its 'scholarly apparatus' is likely to impress lay persons who aren't familiar with the relevant historiography.... Nobody who is familiar with the vast body of archival material on slavery is likely to be impressed by the book's approach. Typically, the author lists the names of eleven Jewish Confederate Navy officers, or the number of Jewish soldiers in the Confederate Army in each state. But ...how large was the army and navy? Ironically, it appears that more Blacks participated in the Confederate Army than Jews! But that's how the book works; the accretion of anecdotes, with no honest attempt to place them in a historical or demographic perspective.[79]

• Selwyn Cudjoe, Chair of the Africana Studies Department at Wellesley College, states:

I think that *The Secret Relationship Between Blacks and Jews* ought not to be used in an undergraduate course on Afro-American history. Their [the Jews'] role was too minimal and their interests too specific (after all, one is talking about individual businessmen rather than the activities of a group) to give it such attention. More importantly, the book itself is offensive to many scholars, Blacks and Jews alike, who find it more a prosecutor's brief (outlining the calumnies of the Jews as Jews) rather than a scholarly attempt to examine the role of individual Jews in slavery and the slave trade.

Furthermore, according to Cudjoe, the book attempts to prove that:

Jewish people... were merely intent, presumably from inherently biological or religious reasons, to participate in the Black African Holocaust.... This would be laughable if it weren't so patently and scurrilously anti-Semitic.[80]

• Abraham H. Foxman, National Director of the Anti-Defamation League, has pointed out how *The Secret Relationship Between Blacks and Jews* follows in the tradition of age-old, anti-Semitic propaganda:

In the process [of publicizing the book], they rationalize and demean the centuries of suffering that brought Jews to the Americas. For example, the book's introduction opens with the observation that 'no single group of people have faced blanket expulsion in so many places around the world as have the Jews.'[81] Rather than attribute this fact to the enduring legacy of anti-Semitism, however, the authors provide a list of reasons for these expulsions: The Jews were monopolizers, usurers, they engaged in 'sharp practices' and sold 'cheap' goods, they filed for frequent bankruptcies. Each of these charges, of course, stems from the timeless stereotype that Jews are inherently untrustworthy and obsessed with money, a stereotype the Nation of Islam apparently accepts as reasonable.[82]

"Jews invented biblical justifications for slavery (The Hamitic Myth)"

Background:

And he said: Cursed be Canaan; A servant of servants shall he be unto his brethren. And he said: Blessed be the Lord, the God of Shem; And let Canaan be their servant. God enlarge Japheth, and see him dwell in the tents of Shem; And let Canaan be their servant."

Gen. 9:25–27

For some years, Wellesley College Professor of Africana Studies, Anthony C. Martin, Minister Louis Farrakhan of the Nation of Islam, and others associated with them have declared in speeches and writings that Jews and Judaism are responsible for inventing biblical justifications for slavery; an allegation known as the Hamitic Myth. According to their argument, Talmudic scholars invented the myth thousands of years ago, "whereby Noah in the Book of Genesis cursed the descendants of his son, Ham, to eternal bondage."[83]

Professor Martin argues that the origin of Jewish involvement in the slave trade in the nineteenth century is rooted in the Hamitic Myth, which, he claims, provided slave dealers and owners with biblical proof that God had cursed Africans to slavery from the time of Noah. According to Professor Martin, the "curse" of Ham was the moral pretext upon which the entire slave trade grew and flourished.

Contemporary Examples:

• In his 1993 book, *The Jewish Onslaught: Dispatches from the Wellesley Battlefront*, Professor Martin wrote that:

> It is the turn of the Jews to retract, apologize, and pay reparations for their invention of the Hamitic Myth, which killed many millions more than all the anti-Jewish pogroms and holocausts [*sic*] of Europe.[84]

• In a speech at Howard University, in April 1994, Martin declared:

> Even though the slave trade was a physical thing... an important part of this genocide has to deal with the intellectual pretexts... used to justify our enslavement.... The most pernicious of all these intellectual justifications for genocide was the Hamitic Myth.... The blame for this Hamitic Myth, which ultimately resulted in the death of 300 million or more of our people... lies with Jewish rabbis, the people who invented the Talmud... a thousand years before the trans-Atlantic slave trade.[85]

• In the June 11, 1996 issue of the Nation of Islam newspaper, *The Final Call*, Marcus Lewis, identified as President of the National African Consensus, wrote:

> Jewish leaders must apologize to Black people for the invention of the Curse of Ham by Jewish Talmudic scholars....

We believe that the Curse of Ham (which claims, among other things, that all Black people are forever destined to serve as the slaves of other races), is the greatest albatross to ever encircle the neck of any people.... While space and time do not allow for a full explanation of this myth and its origins here, suffice it to say that the Curse of Ham was introduced to the world by Jewish scholars....

Not even Hitler's evil deeds compare in magnitude to the genocidal legacy left by this myth of ancient Jewish origin.[86]

Responses:

• Martin's anti-Jewish animus is well-documented in his own speeches and writings. In his book, *The Jewish Onslaught*, for example, Professor Martin invokes timeless, anti-Jewish stereotypes about the Jews' control of money and media. In other writings and speeches, Martin has accused Jews of controlling the slave trade and the international prostitution market, as well as conspiring to control the civil rights movement to the detriment of African-Americans.

• Martin's anti-Semitism has been rejected and denounced by his African-American and White colleagues at Wellesley College. As an example, Professor Selwyn R. Cudjoe, the chairperson of Professor Martin's department, called the trend in pseudoscholarship exemplified by *The Jewish Onslaught* and similar conspiracy-theory books, "Gangsta history, meant to demean and to defame others and to bring them into disrepute, rather than to enlighten and to lead us to a more complex and sophisticated understanding of social phenomena. It ought to be labeled anti-Semitic."[87]

• In an article from the *Journal of the American Academy of Religion*, entitled "The Early Rabbinic Exegesis on Noah's Son, Ham," Wellesley Professor of Religion, David H. Aaron wrote that no justification of slavery exists in the biblical commentaries of Rashi, Abraham Ibn Ezra, the Rambam (Maimonides), and Sforno. Professor Aaron adds that:

There is no Jewish source which condemns the Kushites (Ethiopians) to slavery. There is no ancient evidence, nor is there any medieval evidence suggesting that Jews had any reason to provide a religious or ideological justification of the enslavement of Black Africans.... No sage represented in early or medieval Hebrew and Aramaic literature ever conveys a concern with the policy of enslavement of Blacks as a racial religious policy. Indeed no theological justification is incorporated into Scripture or rabbinical literature for slavery despite the fact that slavery was... a fact of the Ancient Near Eastern world.[88]

• Aaron also documents the following:

In the entirety of the Babylonian Talmud, there is but one reference to a myth which cites a sin of Ham and resulting punishment manifest in his skin [as Blackness]. To place this in context for the nonexpert; the standard English translation of the Talmud (Soncino Edition) is seventeen volumes, with the average volume being approximately 800 pages in length.... It is important to note that this passage... is but one of five different interpretations offered in a string of exegetical alternatives.... No one interpretation is given preference....In assessing the impact of this "myth" we do not find evidence for centuries of Jewish thought in the dictum of a single fourth or fifth-century source. Indeed, what should impress the reader is the *relative paucity of sources reflecting this motif* [emphasis in original] and their rather impoverished development....[89]

• If the Talmud did not originate the "Myth of Ham," as it was applied to African people, where did it come from? In answer, Professor Aaron cites one possibility, raised by Princeton University Professor Bernard Lewis, "suggest[ing] that St. Ephrem, the Syrian Church Father (d. 373 C.E.), may be the earliest source expressing the notion that both Canaan and Ham became Black.[90] Therefore, the Hamitic Myth, the central issue in Martin's indictment of Jewish racism, turns out not to be a Jewish myth at all.

• The Talmud is filled with rejoinders to slavery. The Bible teaches that Jews, because they who were once slaves in

Egypt, have a special responsibility (1) not to enslave others, and (2) to treat any slaves they do encounter as fellow human beings. Several examples follow:

> You shall not turn over to his master a slave who seeks refuge with you from his master. He shall live with you in any place he may choose among the settlements in your midst, wherever he pleases; you must not ill-treat him.
>
> Deut. 23:16,17

> Always remember that you were slaves in the land of Egypt and the Lord your God redeemed you; therefore I enjoin this commandment upon you today.
>
> Deut. 15:15

Confronting Anti-Semitism on a Personal Level

Okay. You've read the anti-Semitic myths and the factual rebuttals to them. Combining history and common sense, you now are intellectually prepared to confront anti-Semitism or an anti-Semite. The strategies involved in effectively presenting your argument have been considered. Methods through which to initiate, maintain, and utilize a diverse coalition of strategies against anti-Semitism have been suggested. Now you're ready—right?

Well, perhaps not. Why? Because it is still difficult for most people to confront another person or group of people—up-close and personal, as they say. It is made even harder when the bigot is a friend, colleague, employer, professor, customer… indeed, anyone you know! That they often don't look or sound like Hitler, David Duke, or Louis Farrakhan won't make it easier.

The difficulty that many of us have when confronting haters or ignorant perpetrators of bigotry is not unique to confronting anti-Semitism. It is partly an issue of human nature. It is a problem that surfaces in all relationships, personal or professional. The failure to assert or defend oneself, or to tell someone they have hurt you, is a common source of stress and conflict. The many best-selling books and audio tapes aimed at improving and enhancing one's self-esteem, assertiveness, and interpersonal communication skills are profitable and successful because they seek to meet a real need in our society and within ourselves. If you're uncomfortable at the thought of standing up and confronting anti-Semitism or any form of bigotry—relax—you're not alone. It's hard to do, it's rarely fun, and it may complicate your life.

Still, it has to be done, and it often can be rewarding. Your intervention can help and comfort the victim. It will make him or her feel less alone. As with other forms of bigotry, anti-Semitism ignored or tolerated behaves like a slow cancer: if untreated, it will grow. If you've gotten hold of this book, you're probably sufficiently bothered by anti-Semitism at least to consider taking action to end it.

The following section provides readers with typical examples of anti-Semitism which require some form of response from victims, targets, and witnesses. How one reacts to them will vary depending upon the situation and the personalities involved. Several possible responses are listed below, ending with the single response (marked with an asterisk) that has proven to be the most effective rebuttal, time and again.

CASE 1: The Friendly Neighborhood Store Owner

Mr. Hawkins is the friendly neighborhood store owner. He has just completed negotiating a tough financial deal with a paintbrush salesman. Frequent customers, Debbie and her mother approach the counter where Mr. Hawkins warmly greets them. He then says, "Did you hear the way I jewed that guy down?"

Possible Responses:

  A) Walk out of the store in a huff and never shop there again.
  B) Confront and condemn Mr. Hawkins for his anti-Semitic remark.
* C) Confront him immediately and explain why the remark was anti-Semitic and offensive.

Rationale:

If you say nothing and continue to shop there you will ensure that Mr. Hawkins will continue feeling comfortable with such statements. If you say nothing and cease to shop there, he may wonder why you are no longer a customer, but he won't *know why*, or even that he made an anti-Semitic remark.

If you criticize him and call him anti-Semitic, he may now know he angered you, and might be more careful, but he might persist in making what he considers an "innocent" remark. However, if you call him on it and explain why the remark reflects centuries of anti-Semitic stereotypes you have stopped him, warned him, and informed him.

You might start by saying, "Excuse me, what did you say?" You can respond by saying, "I'm Jewish, or Catholic, or Protestant (or whatever), and that comment really offends me. Please don't use it again."

CASE 2: The Penny Toss

A group of three students sits in a school stairwell and pitch a penny at Jake Cohen as he walks down the stairs, taunting him with the phrase, "Come on Cohen, you know you want it. Go get it, Jew!"

Possible Responses:

  A) Just walk away; ignore them.
  B) Respond sarcastically to the taunt.
* C) Tell the principal, a teacher, your parent, or someone in authority.

Rationale:

Just walking away and ignoring them might seem personally safer, and no one could fault you for doing so. However, ignoring the problem will not make it go away, and bullies who sense vulnerability often increase the intensity of their harassment.

If you respond sarcastically to the taunters, you may risk inflaming the situation. Humor often helps to deflect antagonism but ridiculing them may provoke them as well. A physical response will not likely be tolerated or useful. Schools often suspend both perpetrators and victims in physical confrontations. The best response is to inform the principal, a teacher, a parent, or someone in authority. One shouldn't accept the "tattle tale" rationale for suffering in silence. What they're doing is wrong, it is anti-Semitic harassment, it violates school behavior codes, and it can even reach the level of a civil rights violation.

Having pennies thrown at you because you're Jewish is a very unpleasant and often painful experience. It is a unique form of harassment, as its roots are in traditional anti-Jewish stereotypes of Jews being obsessed with money—the "Shylock" image. What is a "lucky" penny or a "penny for your thoughts" for most people can be a negative slur to Jews. Pennies are not generally thrown at other groups or individuals. For school-age children it can be a serious and disruptive problem.

If a student is facing this kind of harassment, they will not likely be able to focus on learning, feel comfortable, or enjoy school. It can affect their self-esteem, confidence, and might have a long-term effect.

If you're a parent and find out about such an incident, or if it actually has happened to you, quick action should be taken to stop it. If you're an observer of this form of harassment, you should move to stop it as well. Leaving the burden on a young target to tolerate or respond to it alone is unfair and ineffective.

CASE 3: Vandalism at a Community Gym

Sarah and Megan finish playing tennis at a local community gym. As they head into the locker room, Sarah stares in disbelief at the mirror. A swastika and the words, "Jews! Get out!" are scrawled in red. Her friend, Megan, exclaims, "Oh, no!" Two other tennis players walk in and see it, as well.

Possible Responses:

  A) Erase it, and don't tell anyone.
  B) Inform the manager, who then erases it, and urges you not to report it further.
* C) Inform the manager, the police, and the ADL.

Rationale:

By erasing the offensive language and choosing not to report it, you will reward the anonymous vandal with getting away with the deed. You will also choose to suffer through your anger and pain alone, without holding anyone accountable. If you are neither the victim nor the target, you will, by your inaction, be helping the perpetrator or perpetrators to achieve their objective. Your intervention upon seeing it could prevent others from enduring similar pain and anxiety.

If you inform the manager, and he or she photographs it, shares its existence with others who play there, compares these graffiti to other graffiti that may have surfaced, and makes clear the gym's policy against such conduct, you will have done a service for yourself and the gym's other members.

In many instances, the manager may decide not to respond to the incident. Either way you can report it to local police and the local ADL office. Perhaps you will find that this one incident is not isolated to your particular gym. However, if it is the first such incident, it should still be reported, and a thorough investigation should ensue. Whether it's in a tennis club, office lounge, school room, high-school yearbook, a car, or anywhere else, anti-Semitic and racist graffiti and vandalism should not be ignored.

CASE 4: An Anti-Semitic Extremist Comes to Town

An anti-Semitic extremist leader is coming to your campus or community to march or speak. You are aware of his or her record of anti-Semitism and, perhaps, other bigotry, and you want to do something about it.

Possible Responses:

A) You might join in a protest against the appearance, and seek its cancellation.
B) You can stop supporting the institution where the meeting is taking place.
* C) You can seek and/or provide information about the extremist's record of anti-Semitic remarks and other bigoted remarks through letters-to-the-editor, flyers, or other means of communication. You can join in coalition with other groups objecting to the appearance, and offer factual rebuttals to the documented remarks in question.

Rationale:

Since you want to show your own objection to this appearance and join in solidarity with other like-minded people, you've rejected ignoring it.

While you have every right to protest it and even seek its cancellation, a legal challenge asserting the First Amendment rights of the extremist will often be filed and may prove successful. Making the opposition to extremism a free speech, civil liberties issue is thus counterproductive. It often provides important "legal" allies for those who may be as repulsed as you by the hate but nonetheless will defend the extremist's right to speak. By simply ceasing your support of the institution, you've communicated nothing to the effort to oppose the bigot.

The First Amendment is not a first-come, first-serve right. If you don't use the First Amendment before bigots do, you don't forfeit the right. Use it. Fight back against anti-Semitism and racism with facts and the truth. Where possible, use their own words against them. Those who oppose bigotry have every right to vocally protest what the bigot says. As has been suggested elsewhere in this book, don't assume everyone knows all you do about the record of the hater.

Utilize newspaper ads, media interviews, and flyers to inform the public. Consider strategy guidelines outlined in this book if confronting the extremist in front of an audience. Consult the following chapter on coalition building. You will be more effective if you can initiate or become part of a coalition.

CASE 5: Anti-Semitic Telephone Calls

You arrive home one evening and find a virulently anti-Semitic phone message on your answering machine. In this case, you recognize the voice of a classmate of your child or a colleague at work. Over the next week, you continue to receive harassing phone calls of an anti-Semitic nature. Neither your school principal nor your office manager wants to get involved in your "personal problems."

Possible Responses:

A) Ignore them, and hope they'll go away.
B) Confront the caller yourself or the parent of the child, and let them know you'll report them if it continues.
* C) Notify the phone company, local police, and the ADL, and/or a local synagogue.

Rationale:

In cases like these, it is common to feel scared or angry when someone you know is violating the privacy of your home. Phone calls, anti-Semitic vandalism, and other hate crimes expose the vulnerability of those victimized simply because they are Jewish.

As with cases of racism, ignoring them usually will not make the problems go away. Matters will not grow worse, in most cases, if you respond effectively and report the incident. They will often grow worse if you do not respond. If response (B) might work (i.e., to inform the perpetrator that he/she will be held accountable and will be publicly exposed), then it's worth trying.

However, the most effective response is to report the calls to authorities. They are a violation of phone harassment laws and could violate state and federal civil rights statutes. If you do not know the perpetrator, your phone company will usually agree to trace the calls and share that information with local police or district attorneys. Some phones now have an ability to record the phone number of the most recent caller. Call your phone company for information on this service.

Although it is a matter of out-of-school conduct, school authorities should respond to the problem. They can publicize the crime within the school, issue a strong statement of condemnation, and work with teachers, law enforcement officials, a local rabbi or other clergypersons, and the ADL to tailor an educational response or school assembly. If the school doesn't respond, then it is important to hold them accountable. You can work with other parents, the PTA, local clergy, police, or elected political leaders, such as school board members, city councilors, or the mayor.

If the harassment emanates from a work situation, several responses from your employer are possible. First of all, it is a law enforcement matter which can be prosecuted under relevant state or federal statutes. Employers have a responsibility to create a work climate that does not condone or tolerate harassment motivated by any form of prejudice. If your employer does not stop the acts in question, they may be liable themselves. A union, association, or coalition of other employees should, where appropriate and available, be contacted and solicited for their active support. In cases where the harassment actually takes place on the work premises itself, the case for employer intervention is even clearer.

If you have questions, consult an attorney, the local office of the ADL, or a local human-rights commission, or district attorney's office. Many states' attorney-general's office have a civil rights division or designate at least one attorney with civil rights expertise to respond to cases like this.

CASE 6: Religious Holidays Rights

Yom Kippur is coming, and you notify your employer two weeks in advance that you cannot work on this religious holiday. Your employer implies, or expressly warns, that if you don't appear for work on that day, you will face sanctions or risk being fired.

Possible Responses:

A) You need your job so you decide to sacrifice religious observance and work.
B) Other Jews who work there have decided to work rather than observe the holy day and so you do the same.
* C) You inform the employer that state and federal laws protect your fundamental right to take the day off, without pay. The employer has a legal duty to "reasonably accommodate" your religious observance, unless it causes them an "undue hardship."[91]

Rationale:

Religious freedom is a fundamental principle and right in this country. Economic retaliation for exercising that right is frowned upon by law, unless the employer can prove that accommodating your needs will cause them "undue hardship." In most cases, employers will be able to adjust work schedules, or you can switch shifts with employees of other faiths. Don't surrender your legal rights easily.

Of course, it may seem to undermine your case if other Jews choose to work. However, it does not diminish your right to choose to exercise your own rights and practice your faith as you see fit.

If you are threatened with sanctions or are fired, you have a strong legal remedy. Your local anti-discrimination agency or the EEOC (Equal Employment Opportunity Commission) will respond to your complaint, should your appeal to your employer fall on deaf ears. Again, you should consider consulting with an attorney or the local ADL office.

Conclusion:

There are many variations on the theme of anti-Semitism. The situations described above are reflective of typical incidents Jews confront each day in their neighborhoods, schools, and communities. As with most incidents, Jews and non-Jews alike often witness them and thus could choose to get involved.

There is no hard-and-fast rule that fits every situation. When in doubt, call the police, an attorney, or relevant organizations. Don't choose to endure anti-Semitism alone. If you are not the victim or target yourself, don't let that other person shoulder the burden of responding alone. It's a lonely and intimidating experience to be the target of anti-Semitic harassment, vandalism, or assault. It need not be tolerated. It can and should provoke an effective and constructive response.

Coalition Building

"Thou shall not stand idly by"—the biblical injunction from Lev. 19:16 has great relevance in the effort to confront and combat anti-Semitism.

As this book reflects, numerous approaches exist through which to rebut anti-Semitism. The use of factual and historical information is effective. The development and implementation of counterstrategies are also critical. Obviously, each one of us has the ability to make a difference by speaking out against anti-Semitism and simply refusing to "stand idly by."

Another essential resource against anti-Semitism, and in fact, against all forms of bigotry, is the initiation and utilization of coalitions. A person who seeks to make a long-lasting contribution to confronting anti-Semitism can do so by reaching out, educating, and motivating other people to act as partners in that effort. A coalition that includes voices other than those who are victims of anti-Semitism can have a profound impact on the issue. The leader or primary actors of that coalition do not have to be Jewish. Just as racism will never be defeated if African-Americans and other people of color are left to act alone, the problem of anti-Semitism similarly is too deep-seated and wide-spread for Jews to wage an effective battle against it on their own. Working within a coalition cannot take the place of individual action, but speaking out in conjunction with others of like mind and heart can make a tremendous difference.

An effective coalition must have at its roots a strong commitment by non-Jews—Christian and Muslim, Black and White—who see anti-Semitism, not solely as a Jewish concern, but as a serious problem for all people. Conversely, some Jews intellectualize the issue and hold to the notion that anti-Semitism is not, in fact, a Jewish problem, but a Christian one.

This point is not only irrelevant to those affected or impacted by anti-Semitism, it's like arguing over who had the right of way after an accident has occurred. The inseparable truth is that anti-Semitism becomes a Jewish problem the minute it dictates someone's thoughts, is expressed, or is acted upon.

The key is for people of all backgrounds to come together, speak out, and take action as a unified force against anti-Semitism whenever it occurs. As this book has sought to demonstrate, friends and allies from all spheres of life are available to lend their voices in the fight against anti-Semitism. But, first, they must be asked. The well-intentioned words and policies against anti-Semitism adopted by other groups and religious denominations are valuable only if implemented. If you, as an advocate against anti-Semitism, do not need to go it alone, why do so? Reach out. Involve others. Seek help.

Have Coalitions Worked?

The very use of the word "coalition" evokes historic and nostalgic images of the Civil Rights movement and of a time when legal discrimination in this country finally pricked the conscience of most Americans. The movement was carried out and led by thousands of ordinary and courageous Black Americans, but its success would have been extremely limited without the active support of many White Americans of diverse ethnic and religious backgrounds. Christian clergy, labor unions, and especially, American Jews were prominent at the core of that coalition and were on its front lines.

As a result of the Civil Rights coalition, oppressive and discriminatory federal and state laws were changed. Racist attitudes and apathy about racism in America also changed as Dr. Martin Luther King, Jr., and his partners courageously and nonviolently led the way toward desegregation in this country. Progress toward protecting the civil rights of Black Americans is as unmistakable and irreversible as it was hard earned. Although racism, particularly subtle racism, remains entrenched in America, the multiracial coalition for civil rights positively affected the lives of millions of people—Black and White. Such progress should not, however, be confused with elimination of racism or anti-Semitism.

What is a Coalition?

Webster's defines the word coalition as a "temporary alliance of factions for some specific purpose." Its root verb, coalesce, means to "grow together, or to unite, or to merge into a single body or group." The most fundamental reason for entering into a coalition is to achieve a goal not achievable alone.

When is a Coalition Helpful?

The answer is, always. Effective coalition building is enhanced when it reflects an ongoing commitment to dialogue, honest conversation, and education. A steady and thoughtful cultivation of potential partners—particularly when no specific crisis exists—can strengthen the personal relationships that exist at the core of coalitions. People who know people who need help are more likely to help—it's human nature. It removes the distance between a synagogue vandalism and natural empathy. It makes active opposition to hate more likely. It bridges the gap of isolation and separation that bigotry seeks to perpetuate.

What Can Be Done to Form a Coalition?

Simple efforts by Jews, such as inviting non-Jewish allies and friends to a family Bar/Bat Mitzvah, a Passover Seder, a Sabbath dinner, a Chanukah celebration, or a Holocaust Memorial Service, can help deepen their understanding of why Jews feel so vulnerable to anti-Semitism, and, more importantly, expose them to the positive values and culture that make up Jewish identity and history.

Muslims, Christians, and others who wish to make known their denominational and/or personal opposition to anti-Semitism can sponsor a teach-in against anti-Semitism, write letters, organize a hot-line to generate support in the aftermath of an anti-Semitic hate crime, introduce Holocaust education at some level within their church, mosque, campus chapel, social club, etc., and participate actively in other interfaith and ecumenical activities. Efforts to develop exchange programs for young people of diverse faiths are also known to work. Through this kind of personal, religious, and cultural

outreach, stereotypes break down and misinformed presump-
tions about who the "other" group is and what they believe in
can be changed.

What Should You Know about Establishing a Coalition Against Anti-Semitism?

1. Unless otherwise informed, assume that your potential
partners know little about the history of anti-Semitism and or
how, beyond hate crimes or denial of the Holocaust, it currently is manifested.

Despite the unprecedented access we have to the technology of the information superhighway, it remains a fact that
most of us only take the time to learn about that which most
directly affects us. An Irish-American who expects that wide-
spread news coverage about the conflict in Northern Ireland
means African-Americans or Italian-Americans follow or
understand the conflict, will be sorely disappointed. A
Catholic priest who thinks Jews understand the workings and
hierarchy of the local diocese will be as mistaken as Jews who
believe everyone should understand why Israel is so important
to them.

Therefore, whenever it is appropriate or relevant, an
advocate against anti-Semitism should make very clear why
something or some incident is felt to be anti-Semitic. It must
be defined and explained. The information in this book provides substantive and historical support for that effort.

For example, the attempt by Holocaust deniers to debate
the existence of the Holocaust seems to some observers to be
a free speech issue. As distasteful as it may be for some to
acknowledge that a Holocaust-denial movement exists, those
who do see it as an issue of free speech or academic freedom
cannot be ignored. The information and arguments included
in this book about that issue should be disseminated to them.

Likewise, the effort by some to treat Nation of Islam
leader Louis Farrakhan's anti-Semitism as a sort of "intramural" conflict between him and Jews cannot be ignored. Nor can
his follower's efforts to downplay the Holocaust, promote
Jewish conspiracy theories, rewrite Jewish history within the
Civil Rights movement, and redefine the impact of anti-
Semitism as consisting of no more than "throwing a kosher
sandwich on the floor."[92] Advocates against anti-Semitism

must not assume that others understand the facts and the implications surrounding the statements of Farrakhan and his followers. An effective advocate against bigotry should speak out against all such hateful statements, whether their targets are Jews or members of any other racial or religious group. It's not enough to label him or her anti-Semitic. Explain why.

2. Don't wait for a crisis to occur before reaching out to others, and don't neglect your partners or potential partners during calm or quiet times.

Reach out on a regular basis. Offer support when others are threatened or confronting a crisis of racism, xenophobia, or homophobia. Share meals as friends. Exchange interesting articles or books that will strengthen their understanding of anti-Semitism and your appreciation of their concerns. Find ways to stay in touch.

3. Identify key leadership and partners in other communities.

Coalition partners should be recruited in any way that you can. The most effective community leaders are not always those with titles and offices. Think creatively. Anything that conveys the message that anti-Semitism is not an issue for Jews alone should be attempted. Whether you are affiliated with a church, student organization, or acting solely as a concerned individual, a quick look at local media or even the yellow pages can help you identify likely or potential allies.

In What Ways Can Coalitions Be Helpful?

When identified, coalition partners can be helpful in many ways. In the case of a neighborhood hate crime, for example, try to contact representatives of other groups often targeted by such crimes or who currently face discrimination. African-Americans, Asian-Americans, Latinos, Gays, Lesbians and Christian clergy are among the important groups from which to secure support. Their statements, participation and presentations at rallies along with letters to the editor and other forms of public communications can be extremely helpful. Campus administrators, political leaders, student leaders, academics, etc., are similarly important. Their voices need to be heard on these issues. Victims should not be made or allowed to feel as if they are alone. The more people you can get on record opposing a particular incident or responding to a specific problem, the better.

In a case of Holocaust denial, consider reaching out to historians, as well as Holocaust survivors and American war veterans who were involved in liberating the death camps. Cite German sources who acknowledge the history and responsibility of the German government and people in the Holocaust (see pages 31–32 of this book for sample statements). Broaden the rebuttal beyond Jewish sources.

On the issue of the attempted religious conversion of Jews, reach out to Christian clergy, as well as rabbis. Most mainstream Christians today do not subscribe to the idea that Jews need to be "saved" through conversion and the acceptance of Jesus Christ as the Messiah. Don't merely condemn the problem—or its proponent: turn it into an opportunity for education about religious pluralism and the right to worship as one pleases without encountering harassment.

In the event conversionary pressure is applied in individual situations as opposed to a group effort, similar coalition strategies might be in order after the individual problem is addressed. Harassment in the workplace motivated by religious animus is not legal. It can be stopped.

Seek support from your rabbi and from legal counsel or the Anti-Defamation League. As offensive as such an incident might be to you, remember that the perpetrator, although misguided, may be well-intentioned in his or her zeal. There may be no convincing them that their mission is disrespectful and reminiscent of anti-Semitic ideologies and events in history. By involving others in the effort to explain why the incident is wrong, a broader purpose can be served and the activity can be eliminated.

4. Cultivating a relationship between even two groups can be important for future coalition efforts.

This might be a simple and redundant principle, but sometimes people see coalitions as representing many diverse groups—and only as that. As Blacks and Jews have demonstrated for decades, an effective bilateral coalition is, in itself, a great achievement and requires a lot of persistence, information, outreach and maintenance.

Keep in mind that many groups are both religious and ethnic. This provides important outreach and programming opportunities to build bridges, rebut stereotypes, educate, and activate. For example, most Irish, Italian, and Polish Americans are Catholic. Most African-Americans are

Protestants. Efforts that can jointly explore the ethnic and religious ties that bind people together are a worthy investment of time.

5. Individuals and groups within a coalition need not agree on every issue, every time, for the coalition to be viable and effective. Keep the objective of the coalition in sharp focus. It is not the purpose of the advocate to change the minds and politics of coalition partners on issues other than the one at hand.

In working through coalitions, the activist who seeks one-hundred percent agreement ideologically, politically, or culturally, will usually not be effective. Increased understanding between partners about a particular issue of conflict or a centuries' old problem will not always translate into a full acceptance of other differences or reconciliation of other disagreements. Dialogue between partners will likely promote more profound respect for each other's concerns. This certainly applies to the different theological doctrines of Christians and Jews. When discussed in an informed and mutually respectful manner, it actually advances the building of bridges.

Theological differences among interreligious coalition partners must be respected and taken seriously. These can, but need not, obstruct coalition activity. In fact, working together where interests coincide in specific ways can promote a better and more respectful understanding of those different religious beliefs.

In general, one must determine the priority or theme of your coalition; in this case, it is to fight anti-Semitism. You must consider whether other disagreements over less central issues might detract from your overall objectives. Consider whether your fundamental values are being called into question by other activities of the Christian Coalition, for example, or if you can reach a compromise or consensus on basic concerns and keep working together on this issue. Today's antagonist or neutral player may become an invaluable ally tomorrow. Before you rule out a coalition partner, consider the big picture. How can you be most effective?

In the late 1980s, the Catholic Cardinal of a major city visited Israel, and made some ill-conceived remarks after visiting Yad Vashem, the national museum of the Holocaust. The remarks set off a firestorm of responses from Jews offended by them. But the late Nathan Perlmutter, then the

National Director of the Anti-Defamation League, cautioned the critics that there was no need to treat this "mistaken friend" as an enemy. This judicious appraisal was and is a wise contribution to the art of coalition building.

Coalition strategies require patience and understanding. Working with a coalition partner who disagrees strongly with you on other key issues might take some explaining to those within your own community. An effective activist is a thoughtful one and, barring an extraordinary violation of trust or morality by that partner—such as defending the idea that the Holocaust didn't happen, or supporting terrorism—the goal of defeating anti-Semitism must be kept in the forefront. Bending to the point of working with the "devil" is not a necessary or appropriate coalition strategy. However, excluding someone or some organization that could be valuable on the basis of a less than central issue, without fully considering the implications of their involvement in your priority-battle against anti-Semitism, would also be a mistake.

It often takes courage to speak out and take action against anti-Semitism. There is always some degree of security and safety when a collective voice against injustice and hatred is raised. Coalitions are not only a way to convoke such a chorus, they are also the best way to advance the notion that anti-Semitism, indeed, all bigotry, is unacceptable.

"Finding Someone to Blame: The Anatomy of Anti-Semitism"

by Dr. Leon Jick

Every human society is susceptible to the twin temptations of bigotry and scapegoating. The propensity to find someone or some group who can be blamed for frustrations and failure is present in all ages and places. It may have its origins in primitive man's tribal beginnings, in the suspicion that is attached to the outsider, the different. The inclination persists in the most highly developed and enlightened societies. Nonconforming minorities are always targets of discrimination and harassment. If they carry the stigma of having been historically abused, they are particularly vulnerable.

While the vulnerability is always present, the experience of persecution varies greatly. As a rule, in times of tranquillity and relative prosperity and well-being, scapegoating and bigotry subside and retreat to the margins of society. The malevolent myths and negative stereotypes are not eradicated, but they are repressed to the dark corners and persist only in the underworld of paranoid bigots. A healthy society can accommodate difference and mediate the rivalries and occasional friction that arise between diverse and competing elements. Minorities enjoy relative peace and security and can contribute to the general well-being. Their positive attributes are appreciated and their contributions are recognized and valued.

However, in times of anxiety and decline, of bewilderment, despair and failure of nerve, of economic shrinkage and social dislocation, the temptation erupts to find a scapegoat on whom the problems can be blamed and frustrations can be vented. All too often, bigotry singles out a visible and vulnerable minority for abuse and persecution. The "safegoat" becomes the scapegoat. All too often, as in czarist Russia in the past, and in Eastern Europe today, those most responsible for the problems are eager to divert attention from themselves toward helpless, innocent victims.

This response solves nothing and, in fact, intensifies the difficulties. It diverts attention from the real problems and the attempts to deal with them. It may eliminate a productive element in the society that could contribute to solutions. It spreads poisonous and divisive hatred that stifles tolerance, undermines freedom, and corrupts society as a whole. Almost inevitably, the oppression of a minority escalates into the ruthless suppression of rights of large segments of the society.

Examples of virulent scapegoating and bigotry are found throughout history. An early, well-documented example is to be found in ancient pagan Rome. In this instance, it was the early Christians who were singled out as the scapegoats on whom the ills of a turbulent and declining society could be blamed. Tertullian, a second-century Church Father, describes the phenomenon as follows:

> They conspire to bring odium on good men and virtuous; they cry out against innocent blood, offering as the justification of their enmity the baseless plea that they think the Christians the cause of every public disaster. If the Tiber rises as high as the city walls, if the Nile does not send its waters over the fields, if the heavens give no rain, if there is an earthquake, if there is famine or pestilence; straight-away the cry is: The Christians to the Lions.[93]

In more recent times, the role of scapegoat victim has been imposed on such diverse groups as the Armenians in the Ottoman Empire, the diasporadic Chinese in Indonesia and Southeast Asia, the Indians and Pakistanis in East Africa, the Kurds in Iraq, the Biafrans in Nigeria, the Black Christians in southern Sudan, and, of course, in a variety of settings, the Jews.

Why the Jews?

In ancient times, when the Jewish people lived in their own land, there was no such phenomenon as "anti-Semitism." The earliest description of anti-Jewish persecution is found in one of the later books of the Bible, the Book of Esther. The Jews are "different," visible and vulnerable; Haman, an unscrupulous, greedy minister, is provoked because one of them did not bow down to him:

> When Haman saw that Mordecai did not bow down or do obeisance to him, Haman was filled with fury. But he disdained to lay hands on Mordecai alone. Haman sought to destroy all the Jews, the people of Mordecai.
>
> Esther 3:5

A minority—therefore vulnerable and nonconforming—is "different." Moreover, there is profit, as well as pleasure, in eliminating them. They can be robbed, exploited, expropriated. The ancient tale provides us with a paradigm, a model of bigotry and scapegoating.

Since historical times, when Jews became a widely dispersed minority, anti-Semitism has resurfaced repeatedly. Anti-Semitic attitudes have been persistent. Anti-Semitic actions have not been consistent. The experience is not uniform. There are good times and bad times, ebbs and flows.

The entire record suggests that there is a pattern in the changing virulence of anti-Semitism, and it is this: in good times, times of growth, of development, of openness, of optimism in a society, Jews are welcomed. In new and emerging societies, they bring needed skills and experiences. They participate, they share, they contribute. They live as a tolerated and often, appreciated and valued minority.

But then, in troubled times, times of decline, conflict, shrinking wealth, radical anxiety, failure of nerve, times when the search for a scapegoat who can be blamed for troubles intensifies and replaces the search for solutions, Jews are persecuted, often expropriated, sometimes expelled. In the twentieth century, they were ruined in a technologically demonic, efficiently executed Holocaust that has no precise parallel in human history.

This is an instructive pattern. Ironically, this painful pattern may be one of the secrets to the survival of the Jewish people. Precisely because of this pattern, Jews were time and again driven out of declining and decaying societies and welcomed into emerging and growing societies, where their life and their creativity were revived. A succession of great centers of Jewish life and culture has been created in the Diaspora: Ancient Alexandria, Sassanian Persia, Muslim Baghdad, Muslim Spain, Carolingian France, Christian Spain, the heyday of the Polish kingdom, the Ottoman Empire, and most recently, the United States of America.

But this very extensiveness, in space as well as time, creates another unique dimension to anti-Semitism. When duration and extent, longevity and dispersal, were combined with religious ambivalence and competitiveness, they created a pervasive pattern of prejudice and persecution. The love/hate relationship among Judaism, Christianity, and Islam provided rich soil for prejudice and hatred. Anti-Semitic stereotypes and canards entered the mythology and folklore of Western societies, compounded by economic and social segregation: Shylock and Fagin are but two of the best-known images that pervade English literature from Chaucer to Ezra Pound.

What crimes have not been attributed to Jews?

A child disappears—ritual murder.
A plague erupts—well poisoned by Jews.
A depression—Jewish money lenders.
A heresy or a revolt—Jewish infidels and revolutionaries.

The Jews in Western society have become the scapegoat par excellence—blamed by disgruntled groups, by disintegrative societies. In this century, this role has assumed an added dimension. Anti-Semitism became the central ingredient in a political outlook that became a pattern for reorganizing society. The essence of the ideology is racism—and anti-Semitism has been its keystone.

"Die Juden sind Unser Ungluck," said Hitler. "The Jews are our misfortune." With this distortion and distraction as his motto, he rallied and mobilized a defeated and dispirited Germany and led it on a campaign of war and subjugation that almost succeeded in enslaving the world.

Those who were willing to stand idly by, as long as they thought only Jews were involved, were, in the end, almost swallowed up themselves. Jews, of course, were never Hitler's only victims. Political dissidents, religious dissidents such as Jehovah's Witnesses, homosexuals, the differently abled, women (who were consigned to be servants, not only to their husbands, but to the state), and all non-Aryans—Blacks, Roma ("Gypsies"), Slavs—were on the list of inferiors to be enslaved.

The anti-Semitic smoke screen was the cover behind which total repression hid. The experience of the Holocaust was a reminder that Jews often suffer first and worst, but never only. The treatment of Jews has become a barometer for the health, well-being, and humaneness of a society. Anti-Semitism is an early warning sign—of sickness in a society—of danger to freedom, loss of civility and, humaneness.

Is this still true - is it true even in America?

For Jews, America has been different. There have been no pogroms, and anti-Semitism has never become a major political issue. But, prejudice and discrimination have been persistent and have always erupted in troubled times.

In the early 1920s, during the post-World War I depression, the Ku Klux Klan resurfaced, spreading anti-Catholic and anti-Black venom, as well as Jew-hatred. Racial immigration laws were written to exclude Jews (as well as southern Europeans and, of course, Asians). Admission quotas were adopted in colleges and universities. Restrictions were instituted in professions and in housing.

During the Depression of the 1930s, anti-Semitic agitation increased markedly, reaching a peak in 1938, during the economic slump that threatened to undo the progress of the New Deal years. Father Charles Coughlin, the radio priest in Detroit, attracted a nationwide audience with a message blaming a conspiracy of "international bankers," allegedly Jewish, for the nation's economic woes. Charles Lindbergh, a leader of the America First movement who had accepted a medal from the government of Nazi Germany, accused the Jews of pushing America into war. The ailments of economic and political anxiety produced an outpouring of venomous bigotry.

Not until the return of prosperity and confidence did the overt bigotry subside. The post-World War II period witnessed a breakthrough for almost all minorities. Blacks, women, and Jews entered positions from which they had been excluded.

The postwar period, on the whole, was a period of growing openness of opportunity for all, including minorities. Issues of discrimination were addressed and injustices confronted. In 1946, Yale College finally appointed its first Jewish professor. Soon thereafter, segregation was declared to be illegal; "separate but equal" was branded a myth. The late 1950s and 1960s were a time of prosperity, hopefulness, and optimism. The slogan, which was also a conviction, was: "We Shall Overcome."

A President of the United States had the vision to declare a "War on Poverty." Anti-Semitism was at a low ebb, driven underground. Barriers were not eradicated but they were penetrated, and bigots of all kinds were in retreat.

At the end of the 1960s and increasingly since then, the mood has changed. The removal of boundaries and barriers, which promised to make human beings free, in too many instances, seems to leave them bewildered, imprisoned by anxieties, and yearning for lost certainty and unambiguous answers. The consequences of anxiety and uncertainty are reflected in the abandonment of social causes; the retreat into privatism and careerism; the escape into drugs, cults, and religious fundamentalism; the resurgence of callousness toward suffering and injustice and, inevitably, a resurgence of bigotry. Our society is suffused with a revived sense of endangerment.

America and the whole world are experiencing a failure of nerve. Many problems have proven to be more intractable than anticipated. Proposed solutions are bedeviled by unanticipated consequences that create new difficulties. Technology, which promised liberation from drudgery, brings pollution. Planning, which promised rationality and order, turns out to be stifling bureaucracy. Economic change causes disruption and job loss;, problems of poverty, homelessness, and family breakdown seem to defy solution.

In the face of this climate of crisis and frustration, the ever-present temptation resurfaces: find a convenient scapegoat on whom difficulties and failures can be blamed. All too often, the response is: "Don't confuse me with complex responses which are demanding; give me a convenient scapegoat which is consoling. Give me someone to blame." The narcotic of blame, which is soothing but destructive, replaces the tonic of engagement, which is demanding.

We may be dismayed, but we should not be shocked that long-discredited myths and negative stereotypes of Jews resurface and in some quarters, are tolerated. Even among groups that are themselves victims of bigotry and scapegoating, the malignancy thrives.

How should we respond to anti-Semitism? To rebut the slander may seem to some like responding to the question, "Have you stopped beating your wife?" The answer may place the accused on the defensive and appear to dignify the lies with an undeserved importance. However, ignoring the accusations allows lies and distortion to fester and petrify. Even in the absence of confidence, that facts and evidence can change the minds of bigots, the age-old canards must be exposed.

Dr. Leon Jick , Professor Emeritus, Brandeis University.

Anti-Semitism and Black-Jewish Relations

by Jonathan Kaufman

Of all the manifestations of anti-Semitism in the United States, none has been more troubling to Jews, and to most Black and White Americans, than Black anti-Semitism. Sharing the common experience of bigotry and oppression, allies during the Civil Rights movement, stalwart backers of the Democratic Party since the days of Franklin Roosevelt, Blacks and Jews seemed destined for cooperation and mutual understanding.

From the start of this century, Blacks and Jews were on the cutting edge of American race relations. Jewish contributors were at the forefront of the founding of the National Association for the Advancement of Colored People in 1909 and two Jewish brothers, the Spingarns, served as the NAACP's first leaders. In the late 1940's and 1950's, Jewish organizations helped finance some of the earliest research on the ill effects of discrimination and prejudice—research that was influential in the Supreme Court's decision in *Brown* vs. *Board of Education* to end segregation in schools. The cooperation of Blacks and Jews in the early 1960s set the standard for the great coalition that became the Civil Rights movement. At the height of that movement, three-quarters of the money raised by Rev. Martin Luther King, Jr., and other Civil Rights leaders was donated by Jews, from business executives to ordinary workers. During the Freedom Summer of 1964, two-thirds of the Whites who went to the South to help Blacks to register to vote were Jews, including Michael Schwerner and Andrew Goodman, murdered, along with Black Civil Rights worker James Earl Chaney, by White racists that summer.

Yet, beginning in the late 1960s, Black anti-Semitism has erupted more and more frequently until by the 1990s, anti-

Semitism among Blacks, especially college-educated and professional Blacks, ranks among the greatest concerns of the Jewish community. In Washington, the anti-Semite Louis Farrakhan can summon almost one million Black men for what may not be an anti-Semitic march, but is certainly a march led by an anti-Semite. At Howard University, the country's best-known historically Black college, a Farrakhan follower leads students in a chant:

> Who controls the Federal Reserve?
> The Jews!
> Who killed Nat Turner?
> The Jews!

What are the roots of Black anti-Semitism, and how large a danger does it pose?

* * *

Unlike the Quakers or even the Boston Brahmins, American Jews did not have a history of becoming involved in liberal causes. Before the Civil War, Jews in the South largely supported the status quo—slavery—while Jews in the North by and large opposed it. There were Jews who joined the Abolitionist movement, but also some Jews who were slave owners. But that changed radically with the arrival of boatloads of Jewish immigrants in the late nineteenth century. Suddenly, immigrant Jews saw Blacks as people to be supported, even as fellow victims. In New York, the dominant newspaper of the immigrant Jewish community, the *Yiddish Forward* wrote extensively about Blacks as victims of America's intolerance. Following the East St. Louis riot in 1917 in which thirty-nine Blacks were killed, the *Forward* compared the riot to the Kishinev pogrom in Russia in 1903, when more than fifty Jews were killed: "Kishinev and St. Louis—the same soil, the same people. It is a distance of four-and-a-half thousand miles between these two cities and yet they are so close and so similar to each other. Actually, twin sisters, who could easily be mistaken for each other." Just before Memorial Day 1927, the *Forward* asked indignantly: "Where is the spirit of freedom on which our America is always priding itself? And where is the holiness of the Constitution which is so often mentioned? On Monday, the 30th of May, the American people will decorate the graves of those who fell in the great bat-

"ONE REGARDS THE JEWS THE SAME WAY AS ONE REGARDS THE NEGROES — AS A SPECIES OF INFERIOR HUMANITY."

VOLTAIRE

tle to free the slaves in America, and to free America from the stain and shame of slavery. The slaves are today not free in America; the stain of the shame of slavery is still not evident."

In New York, where Jewish immigrants formed the more militant labor unions, Jewish labor leaders reached out to Blacks who worked even at lower-paid and less-skilled jobs in the sweatshops of New York than did Jews. "You Colored workers are exploited and mistreated in the shops worse than any other group," David Dubinsky, head of the Jewish-dominated International Ladies' Garment Workers' Union, told a rally of Harlem workers in 1934. When Dubinsky discovered that the Medinah Temple in Chicago, where the ILGWU was holding its annual convention in 1934, discriminated against Blacks, he gaveled the convention to order and marched them out in dramatic protest.

In 1909, when the "call" was issued that led to the founding of the NAACP, several prominent Jews were among the signers, including Rabbi Stephen Wise, the leading Reform rabbi in the country. Over the next thirty years, Jewish involvement with and contributions to the NAACP mushroomed. Joel E. Spingarn, an assimilated Jewish professor of English at Columbia, became the NAACP's chairman in 1914 and served on and off in that role until his death in 1939. A year later, W.E.B. Du Bois's autobiography was published, dedicated to Spingarn. Joel Spingarn's brother, Arthur Spingarn, headed the NAACP's legal division, drawing on the expertise of the nation's leading Jewish legal scholar, Felix Frankfurter of Harvard. Louis Marshall, head of the American Jewish Committee, argued on behalf of the NAACP in the Supreme Court, attacking restrictive housing covenants that discriminated against Blacks and Jews. At a time when the cause of Black rights was far from popular, Jewish donors gave tens of thousands of dollars to keep the NAACP on its feet. In 1930, the Great Depression threatened the NAACP's future. William Rosenwald, son of Julius Rosenwald, the founder of Sears and Roebuck, offered to donate $1,000 annually for three years, if four others agreed to match the gift. Four did, three of them Jews—Herbert Lehman and Felix Warburg, financiers, and Harold Guinzburg, head of the Viking Press— and one non-Jew, Edsel Ford.

Jewish philanthropists, especially Julius Rosenwald, became generous supporters of Booker T. Washington's Tuskegee Institute, appearing at fundraisers for Washington in New York and building a network of Jewish donors. Jacob Schiff had Washington screen requests for money from other Black supplicants. Rosenwald set up the Rosenwald Fund to dispense money to build Black elementary schools in the South. Between 1912 and 1915, three hundred schools were built; by 1932, the Rosenwald Fund had established 5,357 schools in the South, serving 663,615 students. By the Depression, an astonishing 25–40% of all Black children in the South were being educated in schools built with Rosenwald's money.

What bound these events together was a recognition on the part of Jews that they could not go it alone. However different their experiences in America were from those of Blacks, many Jews concluded that their struggle for equality and fair treatment was linked to the struggle of Blacks for greater opportunity. In the political universe of many Jews, Blacks were not part of the problem, they were part of the solution. A country which treated all its minorities better—Blacks, Jews, and others—was one in which Jews could thrive. Here, as later in the 1960s, idealism and self-interest intersected.

* * *

It was on plantations in the South, before the Civil War, that Blacks first met Jews. Cut off from much of their own tradition and history, slaves learned Christianity from White preachers and quickly fused it with West African beliefs and practices into—the call-and-response pattern of singing, participatory sermons, and the vibrant dancing of the worshipers. White preachers emphasized tales in the Bible that taught slaves to be obedient to their masters. But slave preachers spoke from a different text. They found more fertile ground in the Old Testament, in the stories of Jewish prophets railing against injustice and oppression, and of the children of Israel enslaved in a strange land. The tale of the Exodus and the emancipation of the Jews resonated strongly. In 1822, in clandestine meetings in South Carolina, Denmark Vesey organized a rebellion of slaves. At every meeting he or one of his comrades would read from the Bible about how the children of Israel were delivered out of the bondage of in Egypt. Then they would sing:

When Israel was in Egypt's land,

Let my people go!

They worked so hard they could not stand,

Let my people go!
Go down, Moses, way down to Egypt land.
Tell old Pharaoh:
Let my people go!

Starting around the time of World War I, the great migration of Blacks to the North began, filling cities like Chicago, Detroit, and New York. In 1910, nine out of every ten Blacks lived in the South and three out of every four lived in rural areas. By 1960, three-quarters of Blacks lived in cities and half lived outside the old slave states. It was here, in the cities of the North, Midwest, and West, that many Blacks met, for the first time, the Jews they had heard so much about in church.

The mixed feelings Blacks drew from those encounters filled their writings and recollections. "The Jewish boys in high school were troubling because I could find no point of connection between them and the Jewish pawnbrokers and landlords and grocery store owners in Harlem," James Baldwin wrote of his childhood in Harlem in the 1920s and 1930s. "I knew that these people were Jews—God knows I was told it often enough—but I thought of them only as White. Jews, as such, until I got to high school, were all incarcerated in the Bible, and their names were Abraham, Moses, Daniel, Ezekiel and Job, and Shadrach, Meshach, and Abednego. It was bewildering to find them so many miles and centuries out of Egypt, and so far from the fiery furnace."

Blacks growing up in the North had an ambivalent view of Jews, shaped by economic contact that almost always put Blacks one step below Jews on the urban economic ladder. Whereas many Jews often saw themselves reaching out to "help" Blacks by extending them credit at stores, giving them jobs as maids, passing on old clothes to their children, many Blacks bristled at the patronizing attitude that they perceived lurking behind every act of generosity. They chafed at the vast economic disparity between Blacks and Jews.

In 1935, when rioting broke out in Harlem, it was directed against Jewish merchants and stores. Roi Ottley, a Black author, writing in 1943, charged that Jews had introduced the idea of installment buying into Black life, inducing Blacks to spend beyond their means, leading to a buildup of resentment and anger. Jewish-owned pawnshops, Ottley said, required

Blacks to leave a suit for a month for a two-dollar loan—and then charged an additional one-dollar storage fee. They drove a hard bargain.

Jews were different from White people. They were often the only White people Blacks knew. There was "Mr. Charlie"—Black slang for Whites. And there was "Mr. Goldberg"—Black slang for Jews. At their worst, Jews were seen as the conniving tricksters who took advantage of innocent Blacks beaten down by the oppression of White society. Jews were seen as the driver on the plantation, the hated middleman who did the White man's dirty work.

Some Jews were perceived as insincere. Under the guise of "helping" Blacks and being their "friend," some Blacks argued, Jews patronized Blacks and exploited them. Despite the well-documented flight of middle-class Whites and Blacks to the suburbs, Jews were often the last to stay in "changing" neighborhoods, and for that they were blamed, while others were not. Jews, too, would leave neighborhoods as Blacks moved in. But they often kept their businesses there: the apartment buildings they had bought, the stores they owned and ran. During the Depression, Black activists in Harlem launched a "Don't Buy Where You Can't Work" campaign. Black leaders approached Blumstein's, the largest store in Harlem, which was owned by a Jewish family. Ottley reported that Blumstein "remained adamant to requests or to persuasion to employ Negroes as clerical workers and salesgirls. As a sponsor of Negro charitable institutions, and as the employer of Negro elevator operators, porters and maids, he explained that he had done his share for Negroes, and refuses to budge an inch in response to demands for more jobs."

Such an attitude infuriated Blacks. It reeked of condescension. Encounters between Blacks and Jews always seemed to involve Jews reaching out and "helping" Blacks, "teaching" them, "guiding" them. Many Black intellectuals ended their flirtation with the Communist Party bitter, not only at the communists but at Jews they felt had treated them condescendingly. "How can the average public-school Negro be expected to understand the exigencies of the capitalist system as it applies to both Jew and Gentile in America… since both groups act strangely like Hitlerian Aryans… when it comes to Colored folks?" asked Langston Hughes, bitter after a feud with Jewish communists.

On the eve of the Civil Rights movement, Black attitudes toward Jews were mixed at best. There were roots of cooperation in Black attitudes toward Jews—the shared feelings of being an oppressed people, the history of Jewish philanthropy, the embrace by many left-wing Jews of unpopular causes, the decency and liberalism shown by individual Jews towards Blacks at a time when most Whites shunned them. There were also roots of division—the persistence of an elder-brother mentality, resentment at Jewish overbearingness, bitterness at ghetto businesses, a belief that Jews failed to live up to their own moral standards.

The Civil Rights movement buried many of these negative images. Led by southern preachers steeped in the story of the Exodus and committed to building alliances, it attracted thousands of Jews as marchers, organizers, lawyers, and fundraisers. The Jewish response to the Civil Rights movement of the early 1960s was extraordinary. Fundraisers from the Federation of Jewish Philanthropies began visiting the headquarters of the civil rights organization, Congress of Racial Equality, to brief leaders on how to solicit money from large givers. Black and Jewish lawyers met in an office of the Leadership Conference on Civil Rights, in a building owned by the Union of American Hebrew Congregations, to begin drafting the laws that would become the Civil Rights Act of 1964 and the Voting Rights Act of 1965. Jewish contributions to civil rights organizations swelled. When Henry Schwartzchild, a former official of the Anti-Defamation League, organized a group of lawyers to go down South to defend protesters during the Freedom Summer of 1964, he began with a list of lawyers provided by the American Jewish Committee. Jack Greenberg, a Jewish lawyer born in Brooklyn emerged as Martin Luther King's lawyer and later, as head of the NAACP Legal Defense Fund. In 1965, when King asked members of the clergy to come to Selma to show support for Black voting rights after Civil Rights workers had been savagely beaten, several rabbis chartered a plane and headed south. In the front ranks was Rabbi Abraham Joshua Heschel, who locked arms with King, and led the march across the Edmund Pettus Bridge from Selma to Montgomery.

Most Jews, like most Americans, were transfixed by the soaring rhetoric of Martin Luther King, Jr. Jews were heartened by King's support for Israel and his denunciations of anti-Semitism. But Jews, like most Americans, were ignorant of the festering anger in the northern ghettos during this time, as well as of the long history of Black nationalism in northern cities, like New York, where Marcus Garvey had been a powerful influence in the 1920s. They also were ignorant of the growing power of Malcolm X and the Nation of Islam, which preached separatism and hatred of Whites, instead of integration and the "beloved community" of Dr. King.

* * *

Two trends fed the eruption of Black anti-Semitism in the late 1960s. First was the growing radicalization of the Black Power Movement. Increasingly, groups like the Black Panthers, the Student Non-Violent Coordinating Committee, and others saw themselves as a part of the "oppressed peoples" engaged in a worldwide battle against whites and "imperialism." This led them into sympathy with Palestinians and other Arab countries allied against Israel. "Anti-Zionism" became for many a thinly disguised front for "anti-Semitism."

Second was the approaching clash between Black and Jewish interests as the Civil Rights movement came north. In the South, Blacks and Jews had faced a common enemy: the bigoted White Southerner who, as Blacks joked sardonically, hated "Koons, Kikes, and Katholics." In the North, however, the lines were not as clearly drawn. Blacks and Jews clashed over affirmative action, quotas, and prominent radical Black leaders who took pro-Palestinian positions that offended many Jewish supporters of Israel. Local and neighborhood issues also highlighted divisions. Nowhere was this clearer than in the bitter Ocean Hill-Brownsville school strike in New York City in 1968–69.

Ocean Hill-Brownsville epitomized the failure of New York to educate its Black students. In 1966, standardized reading tests showed Black twelve-year-olds reading two years behind White twelve-year-olds. Only 8% of New York's teachers were Black. There were no Black high school principals, and only a handful of Black school administrators.

In the South, Blacks hobbled by poor schooling knew where the problem lay—with a segregated school system and White politicians and administrators who refused to give Black schools sufficient money, supplies, and books. In New

York, the problem was much the same, but the face of the enemy was Jewish. New York's public schools were both the historic avenue of success for the city's Jews, as well as the employer of a significant part of the Jewish middle class. By 1967, approximately two-thirds of New York's teachers, supervisors, and principals were Jewish. Many of these Jews were liberal, indeed, many had supported civil rights. But in the battle over New York's schools, Blacks and Jews found themselves on opposite sides.

At the height of the school dispute, a Black school administrator dismissed thirteen teachers, all of whom were Jewish. The largely Jewish teachers union went out on strike. Leaflets began circulating accusing the Jewish teachers of being "the Middle East murderers of Colored people" and "blood sucking exploiters." The Jewish president of the teachers union, Albert Shanker, ordered 500,000 copies printed, to be distributed throughout the city.

Passions in New York exploded. Overnight it changed the debate from one on the merits of the school dispute—over which many in the city, including Jews, were divided—into a debate over anti-Semitism in the Black community. Julius Lester, then a Black activist and radio talk show host, invited a Black teacher from Ocean Hill-Brownsville onto his show to read a poem written by a Black student. The poem, the teacher said, was dedicated to Albert Shanker. It began:

Jew-boy with your yarmulke,
Jew-boy, I wish you were dead.

The sound heard in New York in 1968 and 1969 was the sound of a coalition ripping itself apart.

The years following the late 1960s saw repeated clashes between Blacks and Jews over a host of issues: affirmative action, different perceptions over Israel's ties to South Africa, Israeli-Palestinian relations, the rise of Jesse Jackson, and the emergence of Louis Farrakhan. Despite this anger and bitterness, Blacks and Jews were still able to work together on numerous issues in the 1980s, especially in urban politics. Throughout the 1980s, Jews in the cities were the only Whites who consistently voted for Black candidates running for local office. Many of the new generation of Black politicians, like William Gray in Philadelphia, relied on Jews for contributions and support. Whites typically shied away from backing a Black candidate for mayor. Jews did not. Their support ranged from the 32% who voted for Wilson Goode, the first Black mayor of Philadelphia, to the 75% of Jews who backed Tom Bradley, the longtime Black mayor of Los Angeles.

The support of Jews as "swing voters" was crucial in cities where Blacks made up more than 40% of the population but less than a majority. In Chicago, in 1983, Harold Washington had won 18% of the White vote but 33% of the Jewish vote, although he was running against a Jewish opponent. Those Jewish votes, along with overwhelming support from Blacks, helped give Washington his victory. In 1987, Washington had increased his Jewish support, and his margin of victory.

The importance of the Jewish vote was magnified by the willingness of Jewish Democratic contributors and fundraisers to support local Black candidates across the country. Jews were crucial in electing David Dinkins as the first Black mayor of New York in 1989. By the late 1980s, the power of the Black-Jewish coalition behind Bradley in Los Angeles was so strong that it scared most other contenders out of the race.

But the cooperation in politics could not hide the tensions that still simmered between Blacks and Jews in cities like New York. In 1991, for the first time, tensions between Blacks and Jews broke out into open violence in Crown Heights, in Brooklyn.

On a hot August night, a car bringing home the leader of the Hasidic Lubavitcher Jews who lived in Brooklyn ran a red light, jumped the sidewalk, and struck a seven-year-old Black boy on a bicycle, Gavin Cato, and injured his younger sister. An angry crowd of Blacks gathered. An ambulance from a Jewish ambulance service arrived. Police directed the ambulance to take away the Jewish driver of the car who was surrounded by angry Blacks and was in danger. A minute later, a city ambulance arrived and took Cato to the hospital, where he died. Crowds of Blacks, enraged that the driver of the car was not immediately arrested and that the Jewish driver had been taken away by ambulance before Cato, surged through the streets. Three hours later, a group of Black young people descended upon Yankel Rosenbaum, a twenty-nine-year-old Hasidic Jewish scholar visiting from Australia. "Kill the Jew!" they shouted, and Rosenbaum was stabbed to death. The

Black youth later arrested in 1991 for killing Rosenbaum, Lemrick Nelson, Jr., was acquitted of all criminal charges in 1992. In 1997, after a protracted effort, Lemrick Nelson, Jr., and Charles Price were jointly tried (as adults), and convicted in 1998 of having violated the civil rights of Yankel Rosenbaum.

Four days of rioting followed the 1991 incident. Blacks attacked Jewish buildings and stores, breaking windows, looting stores, and setting fire to cars. They threw stones at Jewish and White passersby. David Dinkins, the Black mayor of New York, hesitated to deploy vast numbers of police to stop the rioting. He and the city's Black police chief, Lee Brown, hoped the rioting could be contained and tempers calmed by restraining the police. Dinkins went to Crown Heights to appeal for calm. Dinkins had been elected as a peacemaker; he was a politician used to finessing differences between groups and harnessing them into a political coalition. In Crown Heights, this strategy proved disastrous. The attacks against Jews continued for four days; Dinkins himself was unaware of the chaos enveloping Crown Heights. It was only when he was booed and jeered by angry Black residents when he visited the neighborhood that Dinkins realized the depth of the problem. Dinkins finally flooded Crown Heights with police and brought the rioting to a halt. But the damage had been done. Dinkins was seen as indecisive and out of touch, with a riot in his own city. Jews dubbed the rioting the first American pogrom. Together with the resurgence of Louis Farrakhan and his attacks on Jews two years later, Crown Heights represented the nadir of Black-Jewish relations.

Ever since the late 1960s, Black anti-Semitism has reared its head again and again—in the pro-Arab comments of Black leaders, in the "Hymietown" imbroglio involving Jesse Jackson, in the riot in Crown Heights in Brooklyn, in the rise of Louis Farrakhan. A new trend has developed among Black students on college campuses: the rise of Afro-Centrism, which charges that traditional history ignored the importance of Africa and Blacks in the development of world culture, science, and politics. At the extreme edge of this movement stands several Black scholars who charge that Jews have played a special role in controlling and putting down Blacks. They use as their text a book called *The Secret History of Blacks and Jews*, published by the Nation of Islam, laden with footnotes and pseudoscholarship, which claims that Jews financed the slave trade in Europe and America. They say Jews controlled the Civil Rights movement and now control the world's finances. In their charges and even their language they echo *The Protocols of the Learned Elders of Zion*, an anti-Semitic tract written by the Russian secret police at the turn of the century, which claimed to transcribe "secret" lectures by Jewish leaders, outlining their plans to subjugate Christians and dominate the world.

The emergence of this academic anti-Semitism and its influence on college campuses is especially upsetting to Jews since many have long believed that education and exposure to the wider world reduce incidents of anti-Semitism. Back in the 1950s and 1960s, when the Nation of Islam launched its first big recruiting drive under Malcolm X, the group focused on ghetto street corners and prisons. Now, their target is university students and Black professionals—the up and coming elite of Black America.

Traditional Black organizations, like the NAACP and the Congressional Black Caucus, have begun to explore ways to work with Farrakhan. Talking to African-American college students, Black professionals, and poor Blacks in the inner cities, it becomes clear why these groups were reluctant to ostracize Farrakhan, despite the concern and anger of many Jews. Like a celebrity rock star, Farrakhan has more fans than followers; few college students or Black professionals flocked to the Nation of Islam after his speeches. But Farrakhan touches a chord in Blacks. He stirs more passion and draws larger crowds than any other Black leader today. Most Black leaders are lucky if they can draw five hundred people to a speech. Farrakhan routinely draws 20,000, and in the fall of 1995, he drew several hundred thousand to Washington D.C. for the Million Man March.

* * *

How should Jews respond to the elevation of the shrewd demagogue and anti-Semite, Louis Farrakhan, and, beyond that, to Black anti-Semitism? The efforts of Jews to resolve this question make clear, not just tensions between Blacks and Jews, but fundamental divisions among Jews themselves and, indeed, within the individual Jewish heart.

The rise of anti-Semitism and Afro-centrism in Black life are undeniable. Farrakhan is a dangerous man. His overseas trip and embrace of terrorist regimes in Iraq, Iran, and Libya indicate his access to powerful and dangerous backers. I myself have become a target of Farrakhan's shock troops, with his former spokesman Khalid Abdul Muhammad attacking me as the "White Jew Kaufman" and twisting quotations from my book, *Broken Alliance*, to "prove" that Jews "financed" the slave trade and "controlled" the Civil Rights movement.

The spread of anti-Semitism and hostility towards Jews among the Black middle class and college students, the very groups that have "made it" in American society, is especially troubling. It is the sight of Farrakhan and his followers being cheered at Howard University and by Black students at other college campuses that chills Jews the most.

Among many Jews these days the mood is fervid and angry. "We know all too well where these words can lead," declared one speaker at a Jewish conference on Black-Jewish relations, his voice trembling with emotion. "Do not tell us that these are only words. For we know that words can kill." At a different gathering, a Jewish woman, a liberal feminist, spoke eloquently of her fear at seeing Farrakhan surrounded by his bow-tied bodyguards. "I looked at that picture on television, and all I could see was Hitler surrounded by his brownshirts."

In less emotional terms, conservative and neoconservative Jews respond to the deterioration of Black-Jewish relations by, in effect, declaring "I told you so." The disillusionment and anger of these neoconservative Jews has been growing ever since the late 1960s, when the rise of Black Power took over the Civil Rights movement and the Six-Day War pushed Israel and questions of Jewish identity to the forefront of American Jewish concerns. These Jews said the alliance between Blacks and Jews was over in 1968, when Blacks and Jews clashed in New York in the Ocean Hill-Brownsville school strike. They said it was over in the 1970s, when Black and Jewish groups clashed over affirmative action. They said it was over in the late 1970s, when United Nations Ambassador Andrew Young secretly met with officials of the PLO. And they said it was over in 1984, when Jesse Jackson first ran for President.

For these Jewish neoconservatives, the answer is simple: bury the Black-Jewish alliance, and move on.

I believe these responses, while understandable emotionally, are wrong.

Far from uniting around Farrakhan, Blacks these days seem to me to be divided and confused. What used to be said about Jews is now true of Blacks: in a room of six Blacks, there are seven opinions. Apart from his anti-Semitism and bizarre numerology, Farrakhan's platform of Black nationalism and economic self-reliance is a dead end. Most Blacks know this, which is why few people joined the Nation of Islam after the Million Man March.

While the Million Man March was organized and addressed by an anti-Semite, it was not an anti-Semitic march. Only 5% of those who attended said they were members or followers of the Nation of Islam. The men who attended said they were drawn by a sense of crisis and despair over what is happening in many Black neighborhoods, especially poor Black neighborhoods. How can we doubt them? For most Blacks, certainly for most poor Blacks, the debate over Black-Jewish relations remains a distant speck on the horizon. Their concerns are far more immediate: jobs, poverty, school, crime, drug abuse, the collapse of inner-city Black neighborhoods. When poor Blacks think of Jews specifically, it is in the context of attacks on Farrakhan and controversies over Black anti-Semitism. For these Blacks the Black-Jewish conflict seems a sideshow, a distraction from the real issues that confront them every day.

If Jews only focus on Farrakhan's anti-Semitism and ignore the genuine concerns of the thousands who marched, they run the risk of playing into Farrakhan's hands. They help create for him the image he wants others to believe: that he is the successor of Malcolm X and Martin Luther King and Jesse Jackson, the de facto leader of Black America.

In our understandable concern over Farrakhan's anti-Semitism, Jews often forget that Farrakhan's targets in denouncing Jews as "bloodsuckers" or slave traders are, not only Jews, but other Whites and especially, more moderate Black leaders. For Farrakhan, anti-Semitism is a political tool to isolate and cast aspersions on political rivals. He comes on as the Black man unafraid to stand tall, unafraid to speak the truth about Whites, unafraid of White power—a well-known role in the Black community. Listen to me, his message goes, because all those other Black leaders—William Gray III, Colin Powell, the NAACP, the National Urban League, your minister, your mayor—are too timid to speak out and tell you the truth.

The real danger is that, in the absence of other credible alternatives to Black despair, Farrakhan's philosophy and hate-mongering will draw a wider audience. The rise of anti-Semitism in poor Black communities should not be so surprising to Jews. As long as conditions of poverty and hopelessness continue, these neighborhoods will be potential breeding grounds for extremism.

"Before there can be better Black-Jewish relations," Leonard Zakim has often said, "their must first be better Black-Jewish relationships." The past twenty years have seen an extraordinary growth of the Black middle class, as well as in the so-called poor Black "underclass." It has produced a new wave of local and state political leaders, as well as national figures like Jesse Jackson. It has produced a vibrant Black church leadership that reaches into both suburbs and inner-city neighborhoods. It has produced influential scholars and thinkers, like Harvard's Henry Louis Gates, Jr., who have denounced Black anti-Semitism and other forms of extremism.

It falls to those concerned Blacks and their Jewish counterparts, the heirs to Martin Luther King's "men and women of good will," to both denounce Black anti-Semitism and to work together to alleviate the despair and anger that breeds it. Let me be clear. We as Jews must denounce Farrakhan and his bigotry. But more than that, we must work to isolate him. If, instead, Blacks and Jews turn away from each other, they will create a vacuum that Black anti-Semites will rush to fill. And then, our worst nightmares will be fulfilled.

Jonathan Kaufman is the author of Broken Alliance: The Turbulent Times between Blacks and Jews in America.

"Anti-Judaism, Antisemitism: History, Roots, and Cures"

by Professor Padraic O'Hare

In this essay, I will define Antisemitism,* distinguish it from anti-Judaism, show the intimate relationship between the two, and link both to ecclesiastical triumphalism, glorification of the Church as the one place of salvation and its hierarch as absolute arbiters of truth. The triumphalist attitude is the linchpin of theological anti-Judaism and often of Antisemitism among Christians.

Definitions

For the moment, I accept as a working definition of Antisemitism that offered by Edward Flannery in the introduction to the 1985 edition of his pioneering work, *The Anguish of the Jews*. For Flannery, three elements constitute Antisemitism: hatred, contempt, and stereotype.[94] We shall see, however, that some of the contemptuousness displayed century after century by Christians toward Jews, as well as some of the stereotyping, is fueled more by theological conviction and not by hatred. This is not to claim that where

---

*Advocates for the use of the term "Antisemitism" (rather than anti-Semitism) include Professor Yehuda Bauer of Hebrew University in Israel. The argument for this new usage is that the prior usage subtly grants the existence of something called "Semitism," in response to which one might well assume a posture of opposition. There is, however, no such ideology or entity as "Semitism." Thus the new usage.

> *"A TRADITION OF THEOLOGICAL AND ECCLESIASTICAL ANTI-JUDAISM CONTRIBUTED TO THE CLIMATE THAT MADE THE SHOAH. WHAT WAS KNOWN AS THE 'CATECHESIS OF VILIFICATION' TAUGHT THAT JEWRY AFTER CHRIST'S DEATH WAS REJECTED AS A PEOPLE."*
>
> **DUTCH CATHOLIC BISHOPS OCTOBER 1995**

there is genuine theological conviction, hatred **cannot also be** present. The purpose here is not to exculpate **Christians or** any other people whose imaginations, language, **and other** images contain and carry anti-Judaism. Nor is the distinction that will be made between Antisemitism and anti-Judaism too fine a point, a bit of Gentile preciousness. Both anti-Judaism and Antisemitism predate Christianity.

For example, in his authoritative study, *The Origins of the Inquisition in 15th Century Spain*, Benzion Netanyahu traces Antisemitism and anti-Jewish stereotype to a tract, "A History of Egypt," written by the Egyptian priest Manetho in 270 C.E. Netanyahu calls the work "the first written antisemitic piece to come down to us from antiquity… [one full of] the most atrocious lies and the most absurd libels." A diatribe occasioned by the alliance of Jews in Egypt with the Persian overlords.[95] But Christianity is unique in that its anti-Judaism is born of theological self-understanding, which is to say its understanding of itself has achieved an orthodox status with vast numbers of confessionalists. The foundation and formulation of the self-understanding of vast numbers of Christians cannot helpfully be reduced in all instances to hatred.

The essence of theological anti-Judaism lies in Christian replacement theology, quite literally Christians' understanding of themselves as replacing Judaism in the affections of God, the Holy One. Mary Boys points to the etymology of the term supersessionism, which names the many tenets of this ideology, noting that it derives from the Latin verb *supersedere*, or "to sit upon."[96] Boys identifies eight tenets which define supersessionism: (1) revelation in Jesus Christ supersedes the revelation to Israel; (2) the New Testament fulfills the Old Testament; (3) the Church replaces the Jews as God's people; (4) Judaism is obsolete, its covenant abrogated; (5) postexilic Judaism was legalistic; (6) the Jews did not heed the warning of the prophets; (7) the Jews did not understand the prophecies about Jesus; (8) the Jews were Christ killers.[97]

Clark Williamson and Ronald Allen speak of theological anti-Judaism in somewhat different terms, though their treatment is consistent with Boys's. In *Interpreting Difficult Texts: Anti-Judaism and Christian Preaching*, they identify six defining features of this oppositive theological idealogy: (1) that Jews and Judaism represent everything bad about religion; (2) that the cleavage between promise and denunciation in the prophetic books of Hebrew Scripture is represented by Christianity (promise) and Judaism (denunciation); (3) that Christianity embodies salutary universal values, and Judaism, destructive particularistic prejudices; (4) that the "Old Adam" (Judaism) embodies law and the letter of the law; and the "New Adam," Christ Jesus, and the Christians embody spirit and grace; (5) that the Jews have been rejected for their crimes; and (6) perhaps their most interesting contribution, that anti-Judaism itself is a comprehensive model for understanding both Judaism and Christianity.[98]

Finally, one of the most detailed examinations of anti-Judaism in the polemical texts of the Christian Scripture and early Church life is Jules Isaac's famous list of eighteen points in the appendix of his historic monograph of 1947, "Has Anti-Semitism Roots in Christianity?"[99] Isaac states the case positively, offering propositions for correcting anti-Jewish stereotyping and ignorance about the Second Testament and the early days of Jewish Christianity. By putting the propositions in a negative key, we have an exhaustive catalogue of the erroneous foundations of theological anti-Judaism.

Isaac's points are these: (1) there is awesome ignorance among Christians of the Hebrew Scriptures, and (2) ignorance, therefore, of the spirituality, the faith path, set out in the Christian Scriptures. (3) Christians undervalue, indeed, dismiss the religious and moral significance of Jewish monotheism; (4) deny the vibrancy of first-century Palestinian Judaism from which Christianity emerged; (5) ascribe the dispersion of the Jewish people after the destruction of the Second Temple to divine retribution; (6) ignore things and take certain liberties, casting many of Jesus' Jewish contemporaries in the worst light; (7) fail to link Jesus and his teaching to Jesus' own Judaism and fail to appreciate the "Jewishness" of Jesus. (8) Related to item (7), Christians ignore the fact that Jesus remained a Jew, "under the law," preaching in synagogue and temple for his whole life; (9) deny that Jesus understood his mission as directed to his own Jewish compatriots; (10) deny the acceptance and receptivity of many Jews to Jesus; (11) assume the Jews of Jesus' time rejected him as Messiah when he was presented to them as the Messiah; (12) assume the Jewish leaders of Palestine represented the Jewish people when, in fact, as Isaac says, they were the "representatives of an oligarchic caste bound to Rome and detested by the people;" (13) interpret certain texts so that Jesus is perceived as rejecting Israel, when, in fact, Jesus always distinguished the people of Israel from "evil shepherds;" (14) falsely accuse the Jews of killing God; (15) assert that those who participated in the death of Jesus had the support of the people; (16) assume erroneously that the Jewish people had a legal role in the proceedings against Jesus; and, (17) assume, erroneously yet again, that all or most of the Jews of Jesus' time resided in Palestine.

The eighteenth in Isaac's list is perhaps the most touching point of this awful catalogue of ignorance and prejudice. Isaac concludes his appendix by noting that even if, as is polemically portrayed at the end of the Gospel of Matthew, there were a scene in which a mob of his fellow Jews screamed to Pilate about Jesus, "his blood be upon us and our children" for Rabbi Jesus, "Father forgive them…" consistent with the traditions of forgiveness Jesus learned as a Jew, would prevail. There would be no justification for centuries of contempt and violence or for a whole intellectual structure like theological anti-Judaism.[100]

So, the foundations of theological anti-Judaism! But for all the destructive consequences of this oppositional ideology, it is not yet Antisemitism. Christopher Leighton's effort to distinguish between the two is instructive. He associates the origins of anti-Judaism with the origins of Christianity; and Antisemitism with modern nationalism and racial theories. But his is a useful analysis, even if one accepts a much earlier date for the origins of racial antisemitism, as Netanyahu proposes.

Anti-Judaism, Leighton writes, "took hold in the early Church as the Christians were struggling to explain the Jewish rejection of those messianic proclamations that centered on Jesus… when Christians were straining to establish their own claim to Divine Election. This defensive posture was bolstered by a replacement theology.[101]

In contrast, Antisemitism stemmed from a revolutionary vision of redemption in which the national character could only be fully realized when purged of the corrupting influences of the "Jewish nation …" [a vision in which] the idea of national character was gradually reinforced by pseudoscientific theories that identified the Jewish people as a degenerate race. Antisemitism squeezed the Jewish people into a biological category.[102]

"…WE MUST NOT LOSE THE PERSPECTIVE THAT, FOR CENTURIES, CHRISTIANS AND ECCLESIASTICAL TEACHINGS WERE GUILTY OF PERSECUTING AND MARGINALIZING JEWS, THUS GIVING RISE TO ANTISEMITIC SENTIMENTS."

SWISS CATHOLIC BISHOPS' CONFERENCE

MARCH 1997

The work of definition is not sufficiently served, however, by leaving matters thus: Antisemitism is hateful; anti-Judaism is a matter of sincere conviction, and, as such, is not an expression of hate, though it is a course of contemptuousness based on, among other factors, stereotypes. In a clear reference to "supersessionist anti-Judaism," E. Roy Ekhart first implies that there are at least two kinds of anti-Judaism, and then labels the theological kind, the supersessionist or replacement ideology, "the Christian crime."[103] One does not have to be a racial Antisemite to hate Jews. Theological anti-Judaism gives rise to hatred and not only to benign hope that Jews will see the light and convert. It is crucial, therefore, to state clearly that theological anti-Judaism gives rise to hateful anti-Judaism and to Antisemitism. Consider one Christian and one Jewish commentator on the connections. First, Bernhard Olsen: "One vital point about this unbelievable cruelty for which we Christians must take responsibility is this: that Hitler's pogrom [*sic*] was but the crown and pinnacle of a long history of hatred toward the Jew, participated in (if not initiated by) those whose duty it was to teach their children the truths of Christianity."[104]

And from Eliezar Berkovits: "Without the contempt and hatred for the Jews planted by Christianity in the hearts of the multitude of its followers, Nazism's crimes against the Jewish people could never have been conceived, much less executed."[105]

Christian theological anti-Judaism and the hateful behaviors and beliefs to which it gives rise must be traced to their most elemental source. And that source is ecclesiastical triumphalism, specifically expressed in this instance in what Eckhart calls "supersessionist triumphalism."[106] For a definition, consider Olsen's words: "Many anti-Judaistic expressions reflect the idea that the Church is the ultimate institution, that to which prime loyalty is demanded and which needs to be defended, idealized, and idolized."[107]

One need not ignore the exceptional progress in Jewish-Christian relations during this generation to acknowledge that progress exists in perilous tension with a steady stream of apodictic claims and oppositive use of doctrine from many Christian quarters. With droll British understatement, Norman Solomon muses, "It may be doubted that the refutation of triumphalism is the soundest foundation on which to base relationships with Christians. Evidently, it makes them feel uncomfortable."[108]

There can be no easy consolation for thoughtful Christians, who embrace responsibility (though not necessarily guilt) for the evil generated by Church triumphalism. Nor can there be forgiveness for institutional Church leaders apart from strenuous effort to excise the disease.[109] There is some relief, however, when one contemplates how the history of contempt could have occurred. Here, it is the great Rabbi Abraham Heschel who comes to our aid. Though the whole hateful reality of Christian anti-Judaism and its links to Antisemitism are unique in scope and outcome, the triumphalism that has fueled that reality is not. Triumphalism is endemic to religion. As Rabbi Heschel says:

> Religion as an institution, the Temple as an ultimate end, or in other words, religion for religion's sake, is idolatry. The fact is that evil is integral to religion, not only to secularism. Parochial saintliness may be an evasion of duty, an accommodation of selfishness. Religion is for God's sake. The human side of religion, its creeds, rituals, and instructions, is a way rather than a goal. The goal is to 'do justice, to love mercy and to walk humbly with thy God.' When the human side of religion becomes a goal, injustice becomes a way.[110]

I. Christian Origins and the Second Testament

There is now a vast literature on the Second Testament and primitive Christianity. Were it to pervade Christian understanding, a more factually accurate picture of first-century Palestinian Judaism—of the Jesus movement as a Jewish movement, of the early evolution of belief about Jesus, and of the nature of polemics in the Second Testament—would emerge, and a Christian replacement theology of Judaism might disappear.

But as Wiliamson and Allen note, this theology, supersessionism, functions as a comprehensive model of Christian self-understanding. It is a classic, born as noted above, of the desire to count for the divine election of the members of the new movement, the movement of Jews called "Christians."

In one of its meanings, one associated with philosophical and theological hermeneutics, a "classic" is a text, person, event, or, in this case, an interlocking set of explanations of the nature of things, an ideology, with "excess of meaning."[111] The profundity of the classic is such that when the text, for example, is encountered deeply by people seeking insight in their concrete, existential situations, new meaning can emerge. The process is primarily one of "dynamic analogy"[112]: Ideas live, stories instruct in conversation with human experience. Such an encounter with a classic text is not primarily a matter of bringing scholarly understanding to bear, though such understanding is not antithetical to this encounter.

In the case of a supersessionist explanation for much of what appears in the Second Testament and much that is recalled and given prominence in the early life of the Church, "classic" takes on a different meaning. Here, we are confronted with a classic orthodox explanation. It is golden; it does not admit of new meaning; it is calcified. It is this classic—supersessionist—explanation that confronts professional religious educators, theologians, and exegetes when they invite traditionally educated Christians to reinterpret the story of the Jews in the study of early Christian origins. Reinterpretation includes a great deal of factual correction.

Added to the power of the supersessionist explanation is an anti-intellectual suspicion of scholarly ideas as they pertain to religion. When this is joined to the deeply oppositional character of religion in its conventual forms (which will be addressed more fully in Chapter II) the work of bringing an accurate portrayal of these times, texts, events and developments—the work of purging Christian religious education of anti-Judaism—is seen as monumental work.

Still, we know a great deal on the basis of which supersessionism must eventually fall. We know that the first followers of Jesus of Nazareth were Jews, who did not understand themselves as leaving Judaism to found a "new religion." We know that for them Jesus, now risen from the dead, was not God but the eschatological prophet sent to herald the end of times.[113] When the world does not end, the belief of the Christian Jews evolves, and Jesus becomes for them the Lord sitting at the right hand of the Holy One. And this belief evolves so that by the end of the period, when the canonical writings are developing, Jesus Christ is understood as the pre-existing divine Son of God. We know that during this evolution, another is taking place, the one James Charlesworth designates as the transition from the "Palestinian Jesus Movement" (ending ca. 70 C.E.) to later "Christianity."[114] We also know a great deal about Jesus' Jewishness, his reverence for the people of Israel and for the Law, and the distinction he always drew, as noted above, between the people and some corrupt leaders. Most important for rectifying anti-Jewish perceptions, we know a great deal about the social context of the anti-Jewish polemical texts of the Second Testament, that, in the words of Philip Cunningham, "a contextual awareness discloses that… polemic is the product of human conflict and does not represent timeless truths about God."[115]

When reconstructing early Christian origins and the Second Testament in ways that are, at once, more factually accurate and more contextually sensitive, and that, at the same time, diminish the influence of supersessionist attitudes, it is instructive to consider the Gospel of John and the Pauline writings among the latest and the earliest canonical writings respectively.

In his essay, "The Problem of 'the Jews' in John's Gospel,"[116] Daniel Harrington notes that the overall portrayal of the non-Christian Jews of Jesus' times is as fools, persecutors, and finally, executors of Jesus. The foolishness of the Jews is communicated through the series of debates that are constructed between Jesus and the "the Jews." The Jews are also depicted as persecuting Jesus and his followers over Sabbath healing, as feared by Jesus' followers, and as wanting to kill Jesus.

Considering the Jews' foolishness, Harrington points out that the debates staged in the composition of John's gospel are a literary device designed to highlight Jesus' teachings. The portrayal of the Jews as fearsome, as persecutors, as desiring and eventually, effecting the death of Jesus—the whole seamless, unremittingly negative portrayal—can be ascribed to the sociological, political, and theological factors rooted in the situation and in the perspective of John and his community.

Harrington ascribes the sociological pressure to depict the Jews in negative fashion to the devastating situation of the Jews after the destruction of the Second Temple (ca. 70 C.E.), and the Roman persecution that followed Jewish rebellion. In the process of reconstructing the religious and cultural fabric of Judaism, four normative views emerge about authentic Judaism and the path it should take. These are: apocalyptic, nationalistic, rabbinic, and Christian. Harrington says: "The composition of John's gospel should be viewed against this background and the rival claims among Jews to carry on the tradition of Judaism. The negative portrayal of the Jews in John's gospel is part of an intra-Jewish quarrel."[117]

Charlesworth agrees with this assessment of the reason for the negative view of the Jews, noting:

> It seems… that the hostile portrayal of the Jews in John was occasioned by a harsh social situation: Jews leveling invective at other Jews. John emerges out of an historical situation marred not by non-Jews versus Jews, but by some Jews fighting with other Jews. If this is an accurate perception, as many specialists on John now conclude, then it is misleading to base a Jewish-Christian dialogue on a document which is the by-product of a social crisis; and it is misinformed, and unjust, to justify distrust of Jews on the basis of alleged "anti-Judaism" in the Gospel of John.[118]

According to Harrington, the political reason for the negative picture of the Jews is the result of the same marginal situation of all the Jews in the Roman Empire after the fall of Masada (ca. 73/74 C.E.). Given their extreme marginality, the loss of even a shred of self-rule, and suspicion and subjugation within the empire, "John and the other Evangelists, to various extents, shifted the responsibilities for Jesus' death from the Romans to the Jews… explaining away the embarrassing circumstances of Jesus' death and connecting the Jews of Jesus' day with the rivals of his own community."[119]

Finally, with reference to John's theological orientation, Harrington maintains that the extremely negative characterization of the Jews is a function of John's own proclivity for "dualistic metaphors." Imagery dominated by the categories of light and darkness, with the non-Christian Jews serving as embodiments of darkness.[120]

With reference to Paul and the problem of supersessionism, we can choose no better guide than Krister Stendahl. In his broadly admired and influential study *Paul Among Jews and Gentiles*, Bishop Stendahl definitively lays to rest an interpretation of Paul's life, ministry, and theology that lends itself so formidably to supersessionism. By the end of Stendahl's treatises, the idea that Paul means to replace Judaism with Christianity, that this is his mission, or that his conversion is of this nature, is effectively repudiated.

Regarding replacement, Stendahl says: "It should be noted that Paul does not say that when the time of God's kingdom comes, Israel will accept Jesus as the Messiah. He says only that the time will come when 'all Israel will be saved' (Rom. 11:26)."[121]

Regarding Paul's own life, his experience on the road to Damascus, Stendahl insists that the idea that this represents a change of "religion" is incoherent. "It appears that a Jew, so strong in his Jewish faith that he persecutes Christians, himself becomes a Christian…. [But] here is no change of 'religion' that we commonly associate with the word conversion."[122] On the contrary, Stendahl argues that Paul's conversion consists in accepting a challenging new mission but not a mission entailing abandonment of Judaism. Paul understands himself as "called" in the same sense as the prophets, identifying himself in Galatians 1:13–16, as Stendahl notes, with Isaiah and Jeremiah, as "called from birth."

Paul's conversion is not from Judaism; his mission is not to speed its replacement: "Serving the one and the same God, Paul receives a new and special calling—God's service. God's Messiah asks him as a Jew to bring God's message to the Gentiles."[123]

Though Paul in the first letter to the Thessalonians is angry and frustrated and cries out that "God's wrath has come upon [the Jews who killed both the Lord Jesus and the prophets] at last (1 Thess. 2:14–16)," Stendahl evokes the mature Paul who says, "Has God rejected his people? By no means (Rom. 11:1)."

The expert contextualizing of the seeming "anti-Judaism" in John's Gospel and the illuminating theological and psychological assessment of Paul and his mission ought to persuade traditionally educated Christians that the image of the hard-hearted and superseded Jews who refused to follow Jesus has no place in a positive theological account of who the Christians are and who they are in relation to the Jews. But given the classic status of this account, its influence is hard to excise. It takes, first, an appreciation that the context Harrington and others are reconstructing is not so foreign to our own experience of rivalry about the orthodox position, and that such interpretations are neither cynical nor reductionistic. Second, it is necessary to be open to the violence done Jews by the supersessionist perspective, and the perspective's corrosive influence on Christianity. Finally, this contextualizing has the desired effect only if one's way of praying and reading "sacred" literature is free of fundamentalism.

Harrington offers a clear and compelling case that placing John in the context of the conflicts of late first- and early second-century Judaism within the empire—bracketing, if you will, the polemic texts so that their negativity is not sacralized—in no way reduces claims about the presence of the Holy Spirit. One needs to see those times as like our own, and, of course, to believe that inspiration is available in our own times. Harrington writes:

> Quarrels within a religious movement are often bitter. In our own day, Jews argue about who is a Jew, Catholics debate about the proper interpretation and implementation of Vatican II, and Liberal and Fundamentalist Protestants repeat the "battle for the Bible." Such modern analogies can help us appreciate the context in which John talked about the Jews. A Jew himself, John wrote in a highly emotional setting in which the future of Judaism was at stake. John was convinced that the Christian way was correct and the early rabbinic way was not.[124]

Whether one accepts the righting of the picture of primitive Christianity and rejects supersessionism depends not simply on scholarly evidence. To a greater extent, it depends on truly feeling the horror to which these distortions led and still lead. Later in this essay, I will sketch an outline of the history of contempt, distortion, invective, and violence emerging from these roots of the classic Christian self-understanding vis-a-vis the Jews. For now, I note simply my own experience as a teacher: though painful for honest and kind Christians to admit as credible, when they allow the history of Christian anti-Judaism and Antisemitism into their minds and hearts, they change.

Finally, the exegetical and theological work noted above, the work of Harrington and Stendahl and so many other richly instructive scholars, means absolutely nothing to a fundamentalist Christian. Biblical fundamentalism holds to direct divine dictation of every part of speech in Scripture and therefore to the doctrine of inerrancy and the proposition that everything in Scripture is as true as everything else. The efficacy of a more accurate depiction of early Church origins and the Second Testament in changing anti-Jewish religious attitudes rests on the capacity of the Christian exposed to such exegesis to discern that the truths of Scripture, as the Second Vatican Council constitution on revelation said, are "the truths of our salvation," the truths that bring "new being," holiness in all its personal and social expressions and effects. There can be no saving truth in the assertion that God—who is love—replaces one people with another. This conduces to xenophobia.

II. Early Judaism Understood

The supersessionist mentality and replacement theology rest on one-dimensional, factually inaccurate, and stereotypical ideas about first-century Palestinian Jews and Judaism. The catalogue of inaccuracies includes these: (1) that a single ruling elite held powers within Palestinian Judaism; (2) that its leaders implacably opposed Jesus and his followers; (3) that all Palestinian Jews waited in a culturally monotone and legalistic mire for a Messiah understood in but one way; (4) that all the Jews opposed Jesus; (5) that the Roman authorities reluctantly allowed them to assuage their blood thirst and kill Jesus; (6) that a univocal and uncreative Pharisaic party gained ascendancy after Jesus' death and, evolving into Rabbinic Judaism, has led Jews subsequently along narrow, legalistic lines.

As the rejection of theological anti-Judaism requires an accurate portrayal of primitive Christianity and a more informed reading of the Second Testament, it also requires some appreciation of the Palestinian Judaism, of which the Jesus Movement was a part, and of the real nature of Pharisaic Judaism.

Of first-century Palestinian Judaism, James Charlesworth writes:

> There was not one ruling, all powerful group in early Judaism; many groups claimed to possess the normative interpretation of Torah, Jerusalem, and Temple... [Palestinian Judaism] also spawned and sustained other varieties of Judaism, most notably the Samaritans and the Essenes. Palestinian Judaism was neither dormant nor orthodox; it was vibrantly alive and impregnated with the most recent advances in technology, art, literature, astronomy.... There were not four sects but at least a dozen groups and many subgroups. We should not think in terms of a monolithic first-century Palestinians Judaism.[125]

A comprehensive reconstruction of Palestinian Judaism of the first century is beyond the scope of this chapter. Let two relatively straightforward corrections serve to make the point. They are simple facts, but they correct destructive Christian errors about the Jews of Jesus' time. They deal with nineteen centuries of Christian assertions that the Jewish people bear corporate responsibility for the death of Jesus, and that the Pharisees of Palestinian Judaism have been the paradigm throughout the ages of religious hypocrisy and legalism.

My own early religious socialization as a Catholic Christian was, to a large extent, free of overt theological anti-Judaism. Despite the fact that I am old enough to have heard the "perfidious" Jews prayed for during Holy Week, the sufferings of Jesus were in every instance, if my memory serves me well, associated with my own sins and shortcomings, not the evil intent and acts of some ancients Jews. I recognize many estimable features of my religious upbringing in Eugene Borowitz's treatment of G. C. Berkouwer's biblical exegesis. Expecting to find pronounced Antisemitism in Berkouwer's writings, Borowitz notes with satisfaction that instead, "he systematically applies a universalizing hermeneutic to passages that speak of the Jews as opponents of the Christ and the Church."[126] I remember this well: "Never mind blaming the Jews for the suffering of Jesus Christ; it is your own sins that nail him to the cross."

At the same time, two scenes from Scripture stand out as vividly as these childhood teachings: In Matthew, "the Jews" cry out, "His blood be upon us and our children" (27:25), and in John, responding to a reluctant (weak-willed, but not evil) Pilate, "the Jews" cry, "Crucify him, crucify him" (19:15). It did seem to me that all "the Jews" were crying out, and that poor Pilate was being bullied.

James Charlesworth makes a simple but important point related to blaming all the Jews for the death of Jesus. He notes that the largest number of Jews living contemporaneously with these events lived, not in Jerusalem but in Alexandria, that perhaps less than 60,000 Jews lived in the Holy City and upwards of 200,000 in Alexandria.[127]

As for Pilate, his image undergoes "softening" as the Christian movement seeks tolerance in the empire, a motive which Harrington notes in his discussion of the context of the Gospel of John, as noted above. Yet in his own day, Pilate was accused of "corruptibility, violence, robberies, ill-treatment of the people, grievances, continuous execution without trial, endless and intolerable acts."[128] Pilate was, in fact, removed as governor of Judea for excess cruelty by, of all people, the brutal emperor, Caligula.

Regarding the Pharisees, of which there are estimated to have been at least seven parties, when we search the literary device of setting them up time and again as foils in conversation with Rabbi Jesus, thus allowing Jesus to give his message, what do we find? In the most historical of the texts of the Second Testament, the Acts of the Apostles, we find only two Pharisees mentioned by name. These are Paul and Gamaliel. Of Paul, Eugene J. Fisher writes (citing Acts 23:6-8 and 26:5), "Paul always considered his claim to having been a Pharisee to be a title of honor… and used methods of reading and interpreting Scripture that appear to have been common to the Pharisees."[129]

The Pharisee Gamaliel cautions the Jewish authorities that the Jesus Movement may or may not be of God. If the movement is not of God, it will perish; but if so, it will flourish, regardless of what the authorities do (5:33–39). Fisher describes Gamaliel as "open to God and God's will, seeking truth, observing the commandments of the Torah, and teaching others the way of God's love by example and saving deeds."[130] Even more pointedly, Fisher notes that Gamaliel's reasoning was typically Pharisaic: "The lives of the Apostles were saved by a classical example of Pharisaical reasoning, which is to say reasoning permeated with piety, wit and compassion."[131]

Can we, as Krister Stendahl asks, "liberate ourselves from the historicism of the first century?"[132] We can if we free ourselves from error regarding the facts of Palestinian Jewish life of the time. But beyond correcting their errors, Christians will have to acknowledge, as the great Rabbi Heschel once said, that "God is not a monopolist," that the Holy One speaks to many people, that many lead comparably holy lives within comparably rich paths of faithfulness. With reference to first-century Judaism and emergent (Jewish) Christianity, Jacob Neusner has provided a clue in his book, *Jews and Christians: The Myth of a Common Tradition*, that after the Second Temple, Judaism was preoccupied with sanctification and Christianity with salvation. The distinction will, I hope, suggest, not only comparable strengths as paths to holiness, but the richness of genuine interreligious dialogue base on reverence for people on paths of faithfulness other than one's own.

III. The History of Contempt

Understanding the full burden for Jews of their history with Christians and the burden for Christians of responsibility and often guilt requires a picture of the steady devolution of relations. This common history begins with separation; becomes disdain; expresses itself in efforts at conversion, isolation, and deprivation; and reaches its nadir in our century with the unique genocidal horror, the Shoah.

Jesus of Nazareth lived and died a Jew; likewise Paul, who understood himself as a Jewish missionary to the Gentiles. The early polemic enshrined in the Second Testament is, not disputation between members of rival religions, but intramural contending over the road of faithfulness for Israel. And yet there is separation in Peter's acceptance of the centurion Cornelius for baptism without requiring circumcision (Acts 10) and in the dispute between Peter and Paul at Antioch (Galatians 2:11–21). A trajectory of separation between Jews and Christians is firmly established at the Council of Jerusalem, at which the acceptance of Gentiles who have not fulfilled the law of Israel is canonized (Acts 15:5–11).[133]

"WITH THE NATIONAL COUNCIL OF THE CHRISTIAN CHURCHES, OUR POSITION IS TO AFFIRM 'THAT ANTI-SEMITISM AND THE CHRIST-IAN FAITH ARE INCOMPATI-BLE.' "

SWISS CATHOLIC BISHOP'S CONFERENCE

MARCH 1997

There is relatively peaceful coexistence between Jews and Christians in the empire for three centuries. Some accounts of Jewish persecution of Christians in these centuries are available, though many of them are suspect, and the historian Marcel Simon maintains, "The few sure cases of active hostility do not, it seems, go beyond the realm of individual and local actions. It cannot be a question of a general conspiracy of Judaism nor of a determining role, but merely of actions of some Jews, who abetted of stimulated, active hatred."[134]

During this period, however, the calumnies that would serve for centuries as rallying cries for persecution of Jews are first articulated. Marcion calls for the rejection of the Hebrew Scriptures as, in Franklin Littell's words, the text of a "particularistic" and "materialistic" people.[135] Cyprian, writing in the middle of the third century, expressed the conviction that the Jews are a punished and replaced people in need of conversion. With chilling foreshadowing, he writes of the "final solution" (though not with such intent): "Now the peoplehood of the Jews has been canceled; the destruction of Jerusalem was a judgment upon them; the Gentiles rather than the Jews inherit the kingdom; by this alone the Jews could obtain a pardon of their sins, if they wash away the blood of Christ slain in his baptism and passing over into the Church, should obey its precepts."[136] Even earlier, in the second century, the most lethal of all anti-Jewish religious rhetoric is expressed. In the middle of the century, Melito, Bishop of Sardis, first says that the Jews collectively are a deicidal people.[137]

The fourth century is definitive for relations between Christians and Jews for centuries to come. As Jacob Neusner writes:

> In the beginning of the fourth century, Rome was pagan; in the end, Christian. In the beginning, Jews in the Land of Israel administered their own affairs; in the end, their institution of self-administration lost the recognition it had formerly enjoyed. In the beginning, Judaism enjoyed entirely licit status and the Jews the protection of the State; in the end, Judaism suffered abridgement of its former liberties, and the Jews of theirs.[138]

There follows the patristic age, a period of detailed elaboration of orthodox Christian doctrine, that achieves classic status, the age of the writings of the great early fathers of the Church. Theological anti-Judaism's fundamental themes are established and solidified in these writings. In particular, three Fathers of the patristic period—Ambrose, Chrysostom, and Augustine—will serve to show in dramatic ways the steady ideological consolidation of replacement theology during this time.

Ambrose was Bishop of Milan; he lived from 339 to 397 and was a major influence on that colossus of Western Christianity, indeed, Western civilization, Augustine of Hippo. Ambrose is associated with one of the most chilling early events or texts foreshadowing twentieth-century events. In Letter 40, Ambrose takes issue with the Emperor Theodosius' intention to require Christians of Callinicun to finance the rebuilding of a synagogue burned down by Christians. Ambrose defends the act, writing that what has been done is not so blameworthy, "and less so when it was a synagogue that was burnt, a place of unbelief, a home of impiety, a refuge of insanity, damned by God Himself."[139]

John Chrysostom (347-407) is perhaps the most often quoted father when giving examples of anti-Jewish rhetoric. In or out of context, his flaying of the Jews is breathtaking. A characteristic passage from the "Oration against the Jews" asserts:

> It is because you killed Christ. It is because you stretched out your hand against the Lord. It is because you shed the precious blood, that there is now no restoration, no mercy anymore and no defense.... This why you are being punished worse now than in the past... if this were not the case God would not have turned his back on you so completely.... You who have sinned against Him are in the state of dishonor and disgrace.[140]

Chrysostom is quoted only a little less often than Augustine. Given his preeminence among the Western fathers and the range of continuing influence of his thought, the violent anti-Jewish rhetoric in Augustine's writings is especially noteworthy. Consider two passages, both from Augustine's "Reply to Faustus the Manichean:"

> The Church admits and avows the Jewish people to be cursed because after killing Christ they continue to till the ground of an earthly circumcision, an earthly Passover.... In this way the Jewish people, like Cain, continue tilling the ground, in the carnal observance of the Law, which does not yield to them its strength because they do not perceive in it the grace of Christ.[141]

> No one can fail to see that in every land where the Jews are scattered, they mourn for the loss of their kingdom and are in terrified subjection to the immensely superior number of Christians.... To the end of the seven days of time the continued preservation of the Jews will be proof to believing Christians of the subjugation merited by those who, in pride of their kingdom, put the Lord to death.[142]

Parallel in time to these writings, there is consolidation through Roman law of the marginal and prejudiced place of Jews in the empire, as well as early and especially violent examples of what will become a pattern of pogrom and expulsion in later centuries.

Through laws passed during Constantine's lifetime, Jews are forced, given the odium of the task, to function as tax collectors, as *decurions*. Considering the ruinous economic situation for the times, through this constraint Jews begin to become associated with the economic plight of Christians.

Constantine also forbids intermarriage between Jews and Christians, for fear that Christians might convert to Judaism, not based on myths of racial purity. Under Theodosius, a century later, it becomes a capital offense for a Christian and a Jew to marry; this code equates the act with adultery.

(If we fast-forward to the twentieth century, we have a bracing view of the continuity of the teaching of contempt and of hatred. In 1913, seven years before being elected to the United States Senate, Tom Watson, a racist and nativist demagogue of the early century, wrote: "Every student of sociology knows that the Black man's lust after the White woman is not much fiercer than the lust of licentious Jews for the Gentile.")[143]

In 413 C.E., a group of monks swept through Palestine, destroying synagogues and massacring Jews at the Wailing Wall. In the following year, after 700 years in the city, Jews are expelled from Alexandria by the Bishop, Cyril. In 425, Jews are required by law to observe Christian feast and fasts and to listen to sermons designed to persuade them to convert to Christianity. The Theodosian Code of 439 forbids Jews to own slaves, thus profoundly limiting their economic options. In 534, the Code of Justinian "further depressed the status of the Jews by discarding many laws protecting their civil and religious rights, while retaining and extending their restrictions."[144] The explicit acknowledgment of Judaism as a legal religion is dropped, Jews are forbidden to celebrate Passover before Easter, and the reading of Torah scrolls in Hebrew is proscribed.

With the turn of the second millennium of the common era, from medieval through early modern times, patterns of expression of anti-Judaism and Antisemitism, echoed with horrifying effect in contemporary times, are set. Broadscale violence is validated in the minds of people by marauding Crusaders. The hateful anger of medieval Christian peasants is fed by fanciful tales of Jewish perfidy and felony, and the peasants' murderous revenge grows beyond the power of bishops and popes to restrain them. Rumors of Jewish acts, such as ritual murder of Christian children, are set in the powerful religious symbolism of liturgical contexts to fortify affective repulsion toward Jews, and is codified in a way that Christians, in small numbers and isolated circles, still practice. Wholesale ghettoizing and special identification of Jews is carried out. The association of the Jews with disease becomes more pronounced. Vast populations of medieval Jews are expelled from "host" countries. The association of Jews with bad blood, which provides a foundation for racial Antisemitism, begins. The use of religious pretexts for exploiting the wealth of some Jews moves forward. And the poisonous view of Jews among German peoples grows.

The medieval period also witnesses the growth of chimera about the Jews, fanciful rumors of evildoing on their part. The most famous of these is the story of young William of Norwich, who disappears at Easter, on March 25, 1144. The

> *"WHAT THEN SHALL WE CHRISTIANS DO WITH THIS DAMNED, REJECTED RACE OF JEWS? THEIR HOUSES SHOULD BE DESTROYED, THEY MUST LIVE IN MISERY AND CAPTIVITY, THEIR BOOKS SHOULD BE TAKEN FROM THEM, THEIR SYNAGOGUES SHOULD BE BURNED. WHAT DOES NOT BURN MUST BE COVERED WITH EARTH SO THAT NO MAN WILL EVER SEE STONE OR CINDER OF THEM AGAIN."*
>
> **MARTIN LUTHER**

rumor is spread that the child has been kidnapped by Jews, ritually murdered, his blood drained and used as part of the Passover meal. A century later, in 1255, young Hugh of Lincoln is rumored to have met a similar fate. Thus arises the "blood libel." Such lies stir violent feelings among the Christian peasantry. They combine with the peasants' preoccupation with the devil and the terror induced by plague to portray the Jew in popular imagery and Christian iconography as the devilish, plague-carrying conspirator who, in league with lepers, poisons all the wells of Europe.[145]

The most famous strictures against medieval Jews enacted by an ecumenical council of the Church are those decreed by the Fourth Lateran Council (1215). As Raoul Hilberg has shown, the decrees and laws promulgated at this council and similar ones, as well as the many regional synods throughout the medieval period, foreshadow the Nazi Nuremberg laws. They place Jews in ghettos, require explicit dress, including a golden "Jewish badge," a reminder that the Jews [sic] betrayed Jesus for gold.

Jews are expelled from England in 1290, from France in 1390, and from most German cities between the fourteenth and sixteenth centuries. Most famous is the expulsion of the thriving, culturally rich Jewish communities in medieval Spain, an act preceded by ten years of the Inquisition. It is in Spain, beginning in 1482 with the Spanish Inquisition, that Torquemada relentlessly pursues the hunt for insincerely converted Jews, Marranos, successfully urging the expulsion of all Jews ten years later so that the disingenuously converted can more easily be ferreted out. Here too, is the idea of *mala sangre*, or "base blood," codified in the sixteenth-century Spanish "laws of purity of blood." This is a significant benchmark in developing ideas of racial purity.

Finally, on the cusp of modern times, the preeminent figure of religion and German nationalism, Martin Luther, compares the Jews to the devil—and now causes us to quake in the light of twentieth-century events in Germany. Raoul Hilberg, historian of the destruction of European Jewry, has said that he did not even know of the existence of Luther's "The Jews and Their Lies" until, as a lieutenant in the United States Army combing through Nazi archives in Berlin after World War II, he found a copy of the text among these records.

Hear Martin Luther:

> We are even at fault in not avenging all this innocent blood of our Lord and of the Christians, which they shed for 300 years after the destruction of Jerusalem and the blood of the children they have shed since then (which still shines forth from their eyes and their skin). We are at fault in not slaying them.[146]

Against this background, German nationalism gave rise to virulent racial anti-semitism, as expressed for example, in Wilhelm Marr's 1879 work, *The Victory of Judaism over Germanism*. And in France, Edward Drumont's *La France Juive* heaps vitriol on French Jews against the backdrop of reactionary Catholic longing for the order of the ancient regime and the charge that the Jews are the chief instruments of French anticlericalism and secularism. In Russia, in 1905, the fraudulent *Protocols of the Elders of Zion* produced. This fictitious document alleges the continuing plan for world dominance of the Jewish Elders.

In *Our Peace*, a well-received Catholic tract published in 1936, the French Jesuit theologian, Gaston Fessard, S.J., in a chapter entitled "The Negative Mission and Mission and Destiny of the Jewish People" speaks of the "murderous race... eternally riveted at the crossroads where the destinies of mankind meet and intersect, in order to point out to passersby the directions of history."[147]

And pronounced Antisemitism is evident in early and mid-twentieth century United States, the theological influences clear, for example, in the rhetoric of William Pellet, the 1936 presidential candidate of the Christian Party: "We Americans now have a political party openly and fiercely anti-Jewish. The newly organized Christian Party now gives us an opportunity to register effective protest to the way in which Jews are taking over our industry, our property, and our money."[148]

In mid-century United States, there is no more instructive embodiment of the lethal interplay of theological anti-Judaism (the teaching of contempt) and rabid Antisemitism than the popular "radio priest" of the 1930s, Father Charles Coughlin. Speaking of the *Protocols of the Elders of Zion*, Coughlin proclaims, "We cannot ignore the news value of their strikingly prophetic nature." Charged with Antisemitism, Coughlin's retort is to urge a Christian front which will not fear being called anti-Semitic because it knows the term "anti-Semitism" is only the "pet phrase of castigations in Communism's glossary of attacks." And finally, of the Jews' spiritual inferiority, he says: "Because Jews reject Christ, it is impossible for them to accept his doctrine of spiritual brotherhood in the light in which the Christian accepts it.[149]

Consider finally the testimony in the extraordinary scholarship of David Wyman, for example, in his chilling study, *The Abandonment of the Jews*, documenting the United States' actions toward Jews during World War II. The instructiveness of Wyman's study of the deep-seated Antisemitism of United States' culture, of our leaders' refusal to rescue European Jews in the 1940s, and of the violence toward Jews in this country throughout the war is heightened by knowledge of his personal response to what his scholarship revealed. Wyman is a son of the American heartland, son of a Methodist minister. Nothing in his upbringing prepared him for what his research revealed. To hear him say that in official, if implicit, American policy during World War II, the rescue of European Jews is considered a "problem," is to confront real, though quiet, moral outrage.

Wyman's meticulously researched picture of virulent Antisemitism during wartime in the United States, as well as what he calls "passive anti-Semitism—uncrystallized but negative feelings about Jews"—is a fitting summary to this brief sketch of the history of the teaching of contempt and its effects. He writes, "It was during the war... that anti-Jewish hatreds that had been sown and nurtured for years ripened into some extremely bitter fruits. Epidemics of serious anti-Semitic actions erupted in several parts of the United States." Wyman sights numerous examples of vandalism, public opinion polls showing broad anti-Jewish and Antisemitic prejudice, and, precisely at the time of the Holocaust, examples of what he characterizes as "a small but noticeable flow of hate-filled letters to government officials and members of Congress" protesting the idea of rescuing Jews: "I am writing to you to protest against the entry of Jewish refugees into this country... Their lack of common decency, gross ignorance, and unbelievable gall stamps them as undesirables even if they could be assimilated into a common society, which they cannot." And: "I see from the papers the 200,000 refugee Jews in Hungary will not live through the next few weeks. That's too Dam Bad what in Hell do we care about the Jews in Hungary. What we want is the refugee Jews brought to this country returned where they come from." And finally: "Are we to harbor all the riff raff of Europe.... The Jews take over everything here."[150]

IV. The Situation Today

The situation today is, of course, immensely complex. This summary will focus—on the negative side—on the continuing ambiguity of Christian leaders regarding theological understanding of Judaism and Christianity in relationship to each other, on continuing evangelical Protestant anti-Judaism, on the conflicts arising in the depiction of Jews in some African-American nationalist movements, and on current attempts to deny the factuality of the Holocaust. On the positive side, the remarkable growth of conciliation between Catholics and Jews and the general deepening of Christian appreciation for religious Judaism are worth noting.

As this essay is being prepared, *The Catechism of the Catholic Church* in English has been selling for several months. As the "Statement on *The Catechism of the Catholic Church* by the Catholic members of the Christian Scholars' Group on Judaism and the Jewish People" points out, the Catechism "asserts the irrevocable nature of the covenant between God and the Jewish people... refers explicitly to Jesus' Jewish identity, and refutes any notion of collective guilt of the Jewish people in the death of Jesus. It speaks of the Hebrew scriptures as revelatory for Christians, and attests to the Jewish background of Christian liturgy."[151]

Still, the treatment of Jews and Judaism, in what may become a widely influential document, is disappointing. As the study group says, "the *Catechism* does not represent fully the developments in Catholic-Jewish relations since the promulgation of *Nostra Aetate*" or subsequent Vatican statements through 1985, nor the heartfelt sentiments of Pope John Paul II. The study group notes: (1) that Judaism is often referred to in the past tense in the *Catechism*; (2) typological interpretation is employed through the text, encouraging the persistence of supersessionist mentality; (3) Judaism of first-century

Palestine is inadequately described, leaving open the continuing possibility of a sacralizing of polemical texts; (4) and the Shoah (the Holocaust) is not specifically referred to, despite, as the scholars' group points out, Pope John Paul II's words in 1986 that "this is the century of the Shoah."

One sees the problem of continuing reluctance to engage religious difference with absolute reverence for the path of holiness of the "other" in Cardinal Joseph Ratzinger's skeptical commentary at a conference in Jerusalem on Jewish-Christian relations. Delivered on February 2, 1994, Ratzinger's talk identifies the scholarly and religious efforts, such as those directed at confirming the Jewishness of Jesus, the culpability in his death of the Romans, and the Hellenistic influences in early Christianity, as efforts "to mollify the issue," rather than to offer authentic insights designed to cure Christian theological anti-Judaism."[152]

Writing in *Explorations*, William Willimon, Dean of the Chapel and Professor of Christian Ministry at Duke University, points to an even more disturbing development in conservative evangelical Christianity. He reports on the gratuitous anti-Jewish features of the *International Childrens' Bible*, published by Word, Inc. in 1988. Willimon notes that the childrens' Bible is "more anti-Jewish than the original of other English versions. For instance, the King James Version renders John 11:53, 'Then from that day forth they took counsel together for to put him to death.' The International Childrens' Bible paraphrase: 'That day the Jewish leaders started planning to kill Jesus.'" Willimon goes on to note numerous similar examples, such as subheadings like "Jewish Leaders Try to Trap Jesus," "The Jews against Jesus," and "Saul Escapes from the Jews."[153]

On another plane are the vitriolic Antisemitic features of certain elements of African-American self-help, pride, and nationalist movements, and of aspects of Afrocentric studies. Luther's tract, "The Jews and Their Lies," is sold at Nation of Islam gatherings, as are copies of the *Protocols of the Elders of Zion*. Professor Anthony Martin of Wellesley College is only the best-known of professors employing the pseudoscholarship of *The Secret Relationship Between Blacks and Jews*, a text noteworthy for proposing that colonial Jews dominated the slave trade. Characteristic of this tragic linking of African-American progress with Antisemitism are the vitriolic statements of Khalid Abdul Muhammad, charges that ring with calumnies of the centuries:

> I called them [Jews] bloodsuckers. I'm not going to change that. Our lessons talk about the bloodsuckers of the poor in the supreme wisdom of the Nation of Islam. It's that old no-good Jew, that impostor Jew, that old hooked-nosed, bagel-eating, lox-eating, Johnny-come-lately perpetrating a fraud, just crawled out of the caves and hills of Europe, so-called damn Jew.... And I feel everything I'm saying up here is kosher.[154]

Despite the viciousness of this rhetoric, the Antisemitic movement that occupies a privileged place of infamy today—indeed, in the whole sorry history of Antisemitism and the theological assertion that has fed it, prepared for it, or conditioned Christians to accept it—is the contemporary movement to deny the reality of the Holocaust. Despite tens of thousands of volumes of documentary evidence, despite Adolf Eichmann's insistence in 1961 that Reinhard Heydrich told him in 1941 that "the Führer has ordered the physical extermination of the Jews," despite Hitler's own words at the end of January 1942 that "the result of this war will be the complete annihilation of the Jews,"[155] there exists in our time a powerful, effective, well-financed, and broad movement in the United States, Canada, and Western Europe to deny that the ultimate expression of the teaching of contempt and the Antisemitism to which it gave rise ever occurred.

One may question whether the potential critical mass of Antisemitic feelings lessens or whether it is only that social legitimization of the crassest expressions of such hatred fluctuates. Still, there can be no denying that since World War II, in the United States and elsewhere, Antisemitism has been reduced and Christian theological anti-Judaism ameliorated to some extent.

During the pontificate of Pope John Paul II, there have been many epochal statements, many moving events—for example, the first visit of a pope to the synagogue of Rome or the profoundly moving commemoration of the Shoah, Yom ha-Shoah, held within the Vatican in 1994. In some ways, a little-reported letter written in 1987 by Pope John Paul to then President of the National Conference of Catholic Bishops in the United States best summarizes the progress and is most touching. In this letter, the Pope's language comes as close as any official Catholic statement has to taking responsibility on behalf of Christians for the centuries of teaching contempt and for the Antisemitism these teachings have generated: "There is no doubt that the sufferings endured by the Jews (in the Shoah) are also for the Catholic Church a motive of sincere sorrow, especially when one thinks of the indifference and sometimes resentment, which in particular historical circumstances, have divided Jews and Christians."[156]

Though progress in stemming theological anti-Judaism should not be overemphasized, it is nevertheless real. Philip Cuningham's study of the treatment of Jews and Judaism in Catholic religious and curriculum materials, which builds on the 1961 study of Sister Rose Thering and the 1976 study of Eugene J. Fisher, is especially encouraging in this regard. Cuningham finds great cause for hope, even while he points out that what flaws continue to exist result from "uncritical use of the Bible" and possible negative influences in lectionary based programs when those programs are not handled with sophistication.[157]

V. What Is to Be Done?

A people whose classic expression of their self-understanding as a religious community is founded on replacing another people must learn nonoppositional religious sensibilities, must learn simply to revel in the joy of experiencing a particular path of holiness without also seeking to disprove or discredit the "other's." Theological anti-Judaism must be rejected, in the words of Williamson and Allan, as contradicting the good news of God's unbounded love and therefore "simply incredible."[158]

What is required is, to use two shopworn words, *dialogue* emerging from a very deep commitment to *pluralism*. But the dialogue, precisely because it emerges from a profoundly pluralistic mentality, is more than polite agreement to clarify and continue disagreeing. It is also more than agreeing to identify a limited agenda of matters about which there is agreement. Many very insightful commentators misunderstand, and sometimes mock, the profundity of the pluralist mentality required to achieve real reverence for the "other," or to save one's people from corruption as well. Norman Solomon, for example, speaks of liberal theologians on both sides, Jewish and Christian, being able to reach, "accommodations" because of their "relativist" positions, "denying that any theology is ultimately superior to any other."[159]

Authentic religious pluralism leads to dialogue that transcends the false civility of reductionstic and antinomian liberals. Rather as Emil Fackenheim says,

> The heart of dialogue is to... risk self-exposure. If Jews and Christians are both witnesses, they must speak from where they are. But unless they presume to be on the throne of divine judgment, they must listen, as well as speak, risking self-exposure just because they are witnesses.[160]

We end this essay with these words of Rabbi Heschel:

> This is the agony of history: bigotry, the failure to respect each other's commitments, each other's faith. We must insist upon loyalty to the unique and holy treasures of our own tradition and, at the same time, acknowledge that in this aeon religious diversity may be the providence of God.[161]

Padraic O'Hare, Professor of Religious Studies, Merrimack College.

Definitions of Anti-Semitism

Anti-Semitism is a problematic term, first invented in the 1870s by German journalist Wilhelm Marr to describe the 'nonconfessional' hatred of Jews and Judaism which he and others like him advocated. The movement, which began at that time in Germany and soon spread to neighboring Austria, Hungary, France, and Russia, was a self-conscious reaction to the emancipation of the Jews and their entry into non-Jewish society. In that sense, it appeared to be a novel phenomenon, since, as the early anti-Semites were at pains to stress, they were not opposed to Jews on religious grounds but claimed to be motivated by social, economic, political, or 'racial' considerations.

Robert S. Wistrich, *Antisemitism: The Longest Hatred*, 1991

The anti-Semitism in its new form, as it emerged from the 1870s, moved the allegations against the Jews and the concepts of their innate disability into the national, and, indeed, the universal, social, and political sphere.... It claimed to clarify the complex and troubling problems of modern man and to reveal the sources of economic crises and poverty, of political conflicts, of societal ferment and war, and, in fact, of all the sicknesses that trouble mankind.... The name "anti-Semitism," which was taken from the Greek, was also intended to endow the ideology with a sort of scientific basis. In actuality, anti-Semitism was never directed against other "Semites," such as the Arabs, but only against the Jews. The new version of anti-Semitism was destined, in the twentieth century, to play a major and distinctive role in the lives of Jews and all mankind.

Encyclopedia of the Holocaust, 1990

The term anti-Semitism was first used in 1879, and seems to have been invented by one Wilhelm Marr, a minor Jew-baiting journalist with no other claim to memory.... Though the name anti-Semitism was new, the special hatred of the Jews which it designated was very old, going back to the rise of Christianity. From the time when the Roman Emperor Constantine embraced the new faith and Christians obtained control of the apparatus of the state, there were few periods during which some Jews were not being persecuted in one or another part of the Christian world. Hostility to Jews was sometimes restrained, sometimes violent, sometimes epidemic, always endemic. But though hatred of the Jew was old, the term anti-Semitism did indeed denote a significant change.... In medieval times hostility to the Jew, whatever its underlying social or psychological motivations, was sometimes restrained, sometimes violent, sometimes epidemic, always endemic. But though hatred of the Jew was old, the term anti-Semitism did indeed denote a significant change.... In medieval times, hostility to the Jew, whatever its underlying social or psychological motivations, was defined primarily in religious terms. From the fifteenth century onward, this was no longer true, and Jew hatred was redefined, becoming... at least in theory, wholly racial.

Bernard Lewis, *Semites and Anti-Semites*, 1986

The term "anti-Semitism" is itself a propaganda triumph. It was coined in the nineteenth century in an effort to distinguish modern secular hatred of the Jews from the more traditional religiously inspired hatred. The religious tradition, fed over the centuries with new devices, techniques, and slanders, served as the basis for this secularized and modernized hatred. Economic, cultural, racial, and national theories and movements embraced the Jew as the explanation for failure, oppression, and evil. This embrace included virtually all historical stereotypes and slanders that had developed over the centuries. The main difference was that persecution and hatred of the Jew now enjoyed a secular and pseudoscientific respectability and was no longer directly tied to religious justification.

Paul E. Grosser and Edwin G. Halperin, *Anti-Semitism: Causes and Effects*, 1983

Anti-Semitism: attitudes and actions against Jews based on the belief that Jews are uniquely inferior, evil or deserving condemnation by their very nature or by historical or supernatural dictates.

Paul E. Grosser and Edwin G. Halperin, *Anti-Semitism: Causes and Effects*, 1983

Although the term "anti-Semitism"—which means "hostility toward Jews"—is only about a hundred years old, the prejudice it describes goes all the way back to Alexandria, where non-Jews resented Jews and the city's Greek writers attacked Jewish customs. In fact, one writer, living around 300 B.C., challenged the claim of the Jews that they had escaped from slavery in Egypt. He wrote that they had in fact been expelled because they were lepers.

Charles Patterson, *The Road to Anti-Semitism and Beyond*, 1982

Anti-Semitism may be defined as any activity that tends to force into or hold Jews in an inferior position and to limit their economic, political, and social rights. It is not simply opposition to Jews because they are different, although that has sometimes been the explanation. It is more often, at least in the modern world, opposition to Jews because they have become effective competitors for the values being pursued by the prejudiced person.

J. Milton Yinger, *Anti-Semitism: A Case Study in Prejudice and Discrimination*, 1964

Anti-Semitism is not an opinion; it is a fulfillment of a psychological need, to emphasize one's superiority. The anti-Semite is a man, scared not of Jews, but of himself, his self-awareness, his freedom, the changes he might face, the world at large. He is a coward that would not admit his being one... the Jew is only a pretext.

Jean-Paul Sartre, *Réflexions sur la Question Juive*, 1962

Anti-Semitism, in its overt form, is the belief that Jews are a pernicious influence in the entire structure of modern life and hence must be effectively removed.

Jacob R. Marcus, *Essays on Anti-Semitism*, 1946

Anti-Semitism can feed only on hatred; it cannot survive without hatred. It has been employed by the political charlatan, by the opportunist, by the witch hunter, and by the frustrated psychopath. Anti-Semitism has been a vicious circle. Anti-Semitism was responsible for repressive legislation, and, thereafter, pointed to the effect of this legislation to engender new prejudice and more hatred. It created the laws of Europe which forbade the Jews to cultivate the land and then charged the Jew with not producing the food which he ate. It enacted the laws which excluded the Jew from the guilds and prohibited [them] from engaging in handicrafts, and then criticized [them] for not creating. It wrote laws forbidding the Jew from dwelling near his Christian neighbors and commanding him to live only in the ghetto, and then charged him with being clannish. It restricted his every opportunity to earn a livelihood, except in petty moneylending and the collection of taxes—the two professions most despised by the overburdened masses. It created a stereotype of the ghetto Jew for the public mind, using a superimposed photograph for this purpose and then urged the masses to hate that stereotype. The masses did not—could not—know the real Jew. They could see only the false stereotype, the "Shylock." The technique for creating hatred of the Jew was perfect.

Sigmund Livingston, *Must Men Hate?*, 1944

Denominational Statements against Anti-Semitism

There is a special obligation for Christians to make sure that anti-Semitism is combated wherever it appears... where the specter of anti-Semitism again haunts the Jewish people... take action against these acts of racism.
World Council of Churches, 1990

Amongst the manifestations of systematic racial distrust, specific mention must once again be made of anti-Semitism. If anti-Semitism has been the most tragic form that racist ideology has assumed in our century, with the horrors of the Jewish "Holocaust," it has unfortunately not yet entirely disappeared.
Holy See Commission for Justice and Peace, 1988

Discrimination and persecution of the Jewish people have, not only deep-rooted theological, but also social, economic, and political aspects. Religious differences are magnified to justify ethnic hatred in support of vested interests.... Christians are called to oppose all religious prejudices through which Jews or any people are made scapegoats for the failures and problems of societies and political regimes.
General Convention of the Episcopal Church, 1988

Whereas, the Christian Church has denied for too long the continuing validity of God's covenant with the Jewish people, with all the attendant evils that have followed upon such denial; therefore, the Sixteenth General Synod of the United Church of Christ affirms its recognition that God's covenant with the Jewish people has not been rescinded or abrogated by

God, but remains in full force, inasmuch as "the gifts and the promise of God are irrevocable" (Rom. 11:29).
United Church of Christ, General Synod XVI, 1987

All forms of anti-Semitism must be condemned. Every unfavorable word and expression must be erased from Christian speech. All campaigns of physical or moral violence must cease. The Jew must not be considered a deicide people. The fact that a small number of Jews asked Pilate for Jesus' death does not implicate the Jewish people as such.
National Conference of Brazilian Bishops, 1984

A serious dialogue of reciprocal love and understanding must replace the "anti-semitism" which, to some extent, still lives on in Christians. The spiritual bonds and historical statements that bind the Church and Judaism condemn any form of anti-Semitism as contradictory to the spirit of Christianity.
German Bishops' Conference, Bonn, 1980

We thus condemn the recent anti-Semitic demonstrations as sacrilegious, barbaric, and anachronistic, alien to our times; for today, more than ever before, there is a crying need for fraternal solidarity and love between all peoples.
Worldwide Proclamation, Archbishop Theolketos of Athens, Greek Orthodox Church

Anti-Semitism is an estrangement of man from his fellow-men. As such, it stems from human prejudice and is a denial of the dignity and equality of men.... This phenomenon presents a unique question to the Christian Church, especially in light of the long terrible history of Christian culpability for anti-Semitism. No Christian can exempt himself from involvement in this guilt.... At the same time, we must pledge ourselves to work in concert with others at practical measures for overcoming manifestations of this evil within and without the Church and for reconciling Christians with Jews.
Lutheran World Federation, 1964

Very few Christian communities of faith were able to escape the contagion of anti-Judaism and, its modern successor, anti-Semitism. Lutherans belonging to the World

Federation and the Evangelical Lutheran Church in America feel a special burden in this regard because of certain elements in the legacy of the reformer Martin Luther and the catastrophes, including the Holocaust of the twentieth century, suffered by Jews in places where the Lutheran churches were strongly represented....

In the spirit of that truth telling, we, who bear his name and heritage, must with pain acknowledge also Luther's anti-Judaic diatribes and violent recommendations of his later writings against the Jews. As did many of Luther's own companions in the sixteenth century, we reject this violent invective, and yet more do we express our deep and abiding sorrow over its tragic effects on subsequent generations.

The Church Council of the Evangelical Lutheran Church in America

Joint Statement on the Occasion of the Fiftieth Anniversary of the Holocaust

Hungarian Catholic Bishops and Ecumenical Council of Churches in Hungary
November 1994

The bishops of the Hungarian Catholic Church as well as the bishops and leading pastors of the member churches of the Ecumenical Council of Churches in Hungary and the communities they are here representing commemorate in piety the tragic events of fifty years ago, when Jews living in Hungary were dragged to concentration camps and slaughtered in cold blood. We consider it as the greatest shame of our twentieth century that hundreds of thousands of lives were extinguished merely because of their origin.

On the anniversary of these painful events we pay the tribute of respect to the memory of the victims. Conforming to the message of the Scripture we all consider the Holocaust as an unpardonable sin. This crime burdens our history as well as our communities and reminds us of the obligation of propitiation, apart from pious commemoration.

On the occasion of the anniversary we have to state that not only the perpetrators of this insane crime are responsible for it but all those who, although they declared themselves members of our churches, through fear, cowardice, or opportunism, failed to raise their voices against the mass humiliation, deportation, and murder of their Jewish neighbors. Before God we now ask forgiveness for this failure committed in the time of disaster fifty years ago.

We look at those, who in that dehumanized age, rescued lives at the cost of their own, or endangering it, and surmounting denominational considerations, protested with universal and general effect against the diabolical plots.

It is a task of conscience for us all to strengthen the service of reconciliation in our communities, for this is the only way for all persons to be equally respected and live in mutual understanding and love.

We have to aim at developing true humaneness, so that there will be no more antisemitism or any kind of discrimination, and so that the crimes of the past will never happen again.

Opportunity to Re-examine Relationships with the Jews

German Catholic Bishops
January 1995

On January 27, 1945, the concentration camps of Auschwitz and Auschwitz-Birkenau were liberated. Numerous people were murdered there in a terrible manner: Poles, Russians, Rom and Sinti people (Gypsies), as well as members of other nations. The overwhelming majority of prisoners and victims in this camp consisted of Jews. Therefore Auschwitz has become the symbol of the extermination of European Jewry, which is called *Holocaust* or using the Hebrew term—*Shoah*.

The crime against the Jews was planned and put into action by the National Socialist rulers in Germany. The "unprecedented crime" which was the *Shoah* (Pope John Paul II, address to the Jewish leaders of Poland, June 9, 1991) still raises many questions which we must not evade. The commemoration of the fiftieth anniversary of the liberation of Auschwitz gives German Catholics the opportunity to re-examine their relationship with the Jews.

At the same time this day recalls the fact that Auschwitz is also part of the Polish history of suffering and burdens the relationship between Poles and Germans.

Already during earlier centuries, Jews were exposed to persecution, oppression, expulsion, and even to mortal danger. Many looked for and found refuge in Poland. However, there were also places and regions in Germany where Jews could live relatively untroubled. Since the eighteenth century, there was a new chance of a peaceful coexistence in Germany. Jews decisively contributed toward the development of

German science and culture. Nevertheless, an anti-Jewish attitude remained, also within the Church.

This was one of the reasons why, during the years of the Third Reich, Christians did not offer due resistance to racial antisemitism. Many times there was failure and guilt among Catholics. Not a few of them got involved in the ideology of National Socialism and remained unmoved in the face of the crimes committed against Jewish-owned property and the life of the Jews. Others paved the way for crimes or even became criminals themselves.

It is unknown how many people were horrified at the disappearance of their Jewish neighbors and yet were not strong enough to raise their voices in protest. Those who rendered aid to others, thereby risking their own lives, frequently did not receive support.

Today the fact is weighing heavily on our minds that there were but individual initiatives to help persecuted Jews and that even the pogroms of November 1938 were not followed by public and express protest—i.e., when hundreds of synagogues were set on fire and vandalized, cemeteries were desecrated, thousands of Jewish-owned shops were demolished, innumerable dwellings of Jewish families were damaged and looted, people were ridiculed, ill-treated, and even killed.

The retrospect on the events of November 1938 and on the terror regime of the National Socialists during twelve years visualizes the heavy burden of history. It recalls "that the Church, which we proclaim as holy and which we honor as a mystery, is also a sinful Church and in need of conversion" (statement by the German and Austrian bishops conferences on the fiftieth anniversary of November 1938 pogroms).

The failure and guilt of that time have also a church dimension. We are reminded of that fact when quoting the witness given by the joint synod of dioceses in the Federal Republic of Germany:

> We are that country whose recent political history was darkened by the attempt to systematically exterminate the Jewish people. And in this period of National Socialism—despite the exemplary behavior of some individuals and groups—we were nevertheless, as a whole, a church community who kept on living our lives while turning our backs too often on the

fate of this persecuted Jewish people. We looked too fixedly at the threat to our own institutions and remained silent about the crimes committed against the Jews and Judaism... The practical sincerity of our will of renewal is also linked to the confession of this guilt and the willingness to painfully learn from this history of guilt of our country and of our church as well. ("Our Hope," resolution of November 22, 1975)

We request the Jewish people to hear this word of conversion and will of renewal.

Auschwitz faces us Christians with the question of what relationship we have with the Jews and whether this relationship corresponds to the spirit of Jesus Christ. Antisemitism is "a sin against God and humanity," as Pope John Paul II has said many times. In the Church there must not harbor aversion, dislike, and even less feelings of hatred for Jews and Judaism. Wherever such an attitude comes to light, they have the duty to offer public and express resistance.

The Church respects the autonomy of Judaism. Simultaneously she has to learn anew that she is descended from Israel and remains linked to its patrimony concerning faith, ethos, and liturgy. Wherever it is possible, Christian and Jewish communities should cultivate mutual contacts. We have to do everything in our power to enable Jews and Christians in our country to live together as good neighbors. In this way they will make their own distinctive contribution to a Europe whose past was darkened by the *Shoah* and which, in the future, is to become a continent of solidarity.

The Victims of Nazi Ideology

Polish Catholic Bishops
January 1995

Half a century has passed since the liberation of the Auschwitz-Birkenau concentration camp on January 27, 1945. Once again our attention is drawn to the painful reality and symbolism of this camp, where more than 1 million Jews, Poles (70,000-75,000), Gypsies (21,000), Russians (15,000), and other nationalities (10,000-15,000) found an atrocious death.

Only a few months into the war, in the spring of 1940, the Nazi Germans created the Auschwitz concentration camp on occupied Polish territory annexed to the Third Reich. At the beginning of its existence, the first prisoners and victims were thousands of Poles, mainly intelligentsia, members of the resistance movement as well as clergy and people representing almost all walks of life. There probably isn't a Polish family that hasn't lost someone close at Auschwitz or at another camp. With great respect we bow our heads before the infinite suffering which was often accepted in a deep Christian spirit. An eloquent example is the heroic figure of Fr. Maximilian Kolbe, who sacrificed his life for a fellow prisoner in August 1941. He was beatified by Pope Paul VI and canonized by Pope John Paul II. His victory, motivated by the Gospel of Jesus Christ, bears witness to the power of love and goodness in a world of outrage and violence.

Almost from the beginning, Polish Jews were sent to this camp, as part of Polish society, to be destroyed. Since 1942, the Auschwitz-Birkenau complex, as well as other camps in occupied Poland, as a result of the Wannsee Conference became extermination camps to realize the criminal ideology of the "final solution," in other words, the plan to murder all

European Jews. The Nazis transported to the death camps Jews from all European countries occupied by Hitler. Not only Auschwitz, but also Majdanek, Treblinka, Belzec, Chelmno, and others were located in occupied Poland by the Germans as places to exterminate Jews, because this was where the majority of European Jews lived and, therefore, such a Nazi crime could be better hidden from world public opinion in a country totally occupied and even partly annexed to the Third Reich.

It is estimated today that more than 1 million Jews died at Auschwitz-Birkenau alone. Consequently, even though members of other nations also perished at this camp, nevertheless, Jews consider this camp a symbol of the total extermination of their nation. "The very people who received from God the commandment 'Thou shalt not kill,' itself experienced in a particular way what is meant by killing" (John Paul II, homily at Auschwitz-Birkenau death camp, June 7, 1979).

Extermination, called *Shoah*, has weighed painfully not only in relations between Germans and Jews, but also to a great extent in relations between Jews and Poles, who together, though not to the same degree, were the victims of Nazi ideology. Because they lived in close proximity, they became involuntary witnesses to the extermination of Jews. Regretfully, it has to be stated that for many years Auschwitz-Birkenau was treated by the communist regime almost entirely in terms of anti-fascist struggle that did not help to convey the extent of the extermination of Jews.

It must be underlined that Poles and Jews have lived in this country for centuries, and although now and again conflicts did arise, they considered it their homeland. Driven out of western Europe, Jews found refuge in Poland. Consequently, Poland often had the reputation of being *paradisus Judaerorum* ("a Jewish paradise"), because here they could live according to their customs, religion, and culture. Contrary to many European countries, until the time of World War II, Jews were never driven out of Poland. About 80 percent of Jews living in the world today can trace their descent through their parents and/or grandparents to roots in Poland.

The loss of Polish independence and Poland's partition by Russia, Austria, and Prussia - which lasted more than 120 years - brought about, in the midst of other dramatic consequences, a deterioration in Polish-Jewish relations. In the period of time between World War I and World War II, when Poland, after regaining her independence in 1918, sought to find forms of her own identity, new conflicts arose. Their underlying factors were of psychological, economic, political and religious nature but never racist. Despite the antisemitism of some circles, shortly before the outbreak of World War II, when Hitler's repressions intensified, it was Poland that accepted thousands of Jews from Germany.

Seeing the Nazi extermination of Jews, many Poles reacted with heroic courage and sacrifice, risking their lives and that of their families. The virtues of the Gospel and solidarity with the suffering and the persecuted motivated almost every convent in the general government to give Jewish children refuge. Many Poles lost their lives, in defiance of threats of the death penalty with regard to themselves and their family members, because they dared to shelter Jews. It should be mentioned that, as a consequence of giving refuge to Jews, the rule of common responsibility was applied to Poles. Often whole families, from children to grandparents, were killed for harboring Jews. In acknowledgment of this, thousands were awarded with medals "righteous among the nations of the world." Nameless others also brought help.

Unfortunately, there were also those who were capable of actions unworthy of being called Christians. There were those who not only blackmailed, but also gave away Jews in hiding into German hands. Nothing can justify such attitudes, though the inhumane time of war and the cruelty of the Nazis led to Jews, themselves tormented by the occupier, being forced to hand over their brother into the hands of the Germans. Once again, we recall the words of the Polish bishops' pastoral letter that was read at all Catholic churches and chapels on January 20, 1991, which stated: "In spite of numerous heroic examples of Polish Christians, there were those who remained indifferent to that inconceivable tragedy. In particular, we mourn the fact that there were also those among Catholics who in some way had contributed to the death of Jews. They will forever remain a source of remorse in the social dimension."

The creators of Auschwitz were the Nazi Germans, not Poles. Everything that symbolizes this death camp is a result of a National Socialist ideology that was not born in Poland.

Another totalitarian system, similar to the Nazi, which was communism, gathered many millions in a harvest of death. Nazism also meant trampling on the dignity of the human being as an image of God. There existed a dramatic community of fate between Poles and Jews in constraint and ruthless extermination. However, it was the Jews who became the victims of the Nazi plan of systematic and total liquidation. "An insane ideology decided on this plan in the name of a wretched form of fascism and carried it out mercilessly" (John Paul II, beatification of Edith Stein, Cologne, Germany, May 1, 1987).

The world in which the cruelties of Auschwitz were carried out was also a world redeemed and at the same time a world of challenge, even after the *Shoah*, from where arises the message to all Christians that they should reveal God in their actions and not contribute to the questioning of his presence. God was and continues to be everywhere. What is satanic and represents hatred never originates from God but from man, who submits himself to the influence of the Evil One and doesn't respect the dignity of the human being or God's commandments.

The half century that has passed since the liberation of Auschwitz-Birkenau obliges us to express a clear objection to all signs of disregard for human dignity such as racism, anti-semitism, xenophobia, and anti-Polish attitudes. Living in a country marked with the burden of a horrible event called Shoah, with Edith Stein, who died at Auschwitz because she was a Jew, with faith and total confidence in God, the Father of all humanity, we emphatically repeat: Hatred will never have the last word in this world (John Paul II's message prior to visiting the Federal Republic of Germany, April 25, 1987).

The only guarantee of this is to educate future generations in the spirit of mutual respect, tolerance, and love according to the recommendations contained in the Holy See's *Notes on the Correct Way to Present the Jews and Judaism in Preaching and Catechesis in the Catholic Church* (June 24, 1985).

Supported by One Root: Our Relationship to Judaism

Dutch Catholic Bishops
October 1995

For Christians, the Jewish religion has an essential and permanent meaning. This fundamental insight was formally articulated thirty years ago, on October 28, 1965, by the Second Vatican Council in the declaration *Nostra Aetate*. It showed that the Church cannot understand itself correctly when it ignores its relationship to Judaism.

Nostra Aetate stimulated a continuous development in the relationship between the Roman Catholic Church and Judaism. One of the ways in which this is expressed is in the Holy See's official recognition of the State of Israel and the establishment of reciprocal diplomatic relations. On that occasion the Roman Catholic Church expressly defined the obligation to combat every form of antisemitism.

Consistent with this development is the honest reflection on their own history that recently led the Polish and German bishops to recognize co-responsibility for the persecution of the Jews in the past. In all sincerity we join them in this sentiment.

Shoah

In the same way that we are filled with gratitude this year when we recall the end of the War, we are also filled with shame and dismay when we recall the *Shoah*. Literally, this Hebrew word means "catastrophe." It has come to refer to the murder perpetrated on the Jewish people in those parts of Europe occupied by Germany in the years 1933 to 1945.

From our country the second highest percentage of Jews was deported and murdered. This thought holds us in its grasp.

Looking back on the attitude of Dutch Catholics during the war, our thoughts turn to the courageous actions of the episcopacy then led by Archbishop J. de Jong. The occupiers punished this action by deporting and murdering Catholics of Jewish origin, among whom the Blessed Edith Stein. Others also witnessed in their resistance against the persecution of the Jews to authentic humanity and Christian faith.

Errors

But could Catholics not have done more? Were they not required to do more? These questions are too general to answer. The history of the twenty-century long relationship between Jews and Christians is very complex and has left many traces of its passing. There is no doubt that church institutions have made errors.

A tradition of theological and ecclesiastical anti-Judaism contributed to the climate that made the *Shoah*. What was known as the "catechesis of vilification" taught that Jewry after Christ's death was rejected as a people.

Partly due to these traditions, Catholics in our country sometimes were reserved toward Jews, and sometimes indifferent or ill-disposed. Just after the war this was still apparent on the return of those who has been hidden from or who had survived the concentration camps.

We reject this tradition of ecclesiastical anti-Judaism and deeply regret its horrible results. With our pope and other episcopal conferences, we condemn every form of anti-semitism as a sin against God and humanity.

Change of Attitude

In thirty years since *Nostra Aetate*, our Church has undergone a fortuitous change of attitude. A dialogue has been initiated between representatives of Judaism and Christianity. In it Christians become more familiar with how Judaism sees itself, in its tradition and in its present situation, while Jews better understand who Jesus Christ is for us Christians. We rejoice in the results of this approach. But there is still much to do. Prejudice and forms of antisemitism arise repeatedly in our society. This demands vigilance and decisiveness. Our Church has thus taken several initiatives.

In 1951 the Katholieke Radd voor Israel (Catholic Council for Israel) was established with the purpose of increasing awareness in our Church of the meaning of Judaism and improving our relationship. Last year we gave this council official status as an independent church institution.

In addition, we inaugurated last year an episcopal commission for relations with Judaism which is intended to support the policy of the bishops' conference in this area. We appreciate the increased attention devoted to Judaism in Catholic theological education - not only in its historical meaning but also in its present form and the meaning it has now for the Christian tradition.

The dialogue between Christian Churches and Judaism has received a fixed form in the Netherlands in the Overlegorgaan van Joden en Christenen (Consultative Organization for Jews and Christians, OJEC). Via the Katholieke Raad voor Israel (Catholic Council for Israel), our Church participates in this organization.

Vitally Linked

Neither condemnation nor vilification, but respect and humility must determine our attitude to Judaism's role in God's history among people.

We Christians may never forget that Jesus of Nazareth is a son of the Jewish people, rooted in the tradition of Moses and the prophets. In meeting Judaism, we will better understand Jesus. In the scriptures, but also in our theology and liturgy, we remain vitally linked with the Jewish religion. Jews and Christians are sustained by the same root.

The more our actions are grounded in that awareness, the more we will contribute to the *shalom* promised to all peoples. We appeal to everyone to adopt the words Paul addressed to the Christians of Rome: "If the root is holy, so are the branches. But if some of the branches were broken off, and you, a wild olive shoot, were grafted in their place and have come to share the rich root of the olive tree, do no boast against the branches. If you do boast, consider that you do not support the root; the root supports you" (Roman 11:16-18).

Confronting the Debate About the Role of Switzerland During the Second World War

Swiss Catholic Bishops' Conference
March 1997

The Bishops' Conference hereby contribute a study to the current debate in our country. The role of Switzerland during the Second World War has become the object of fierce debate. It is necessary to state that this role is appreciated very differently today by the generation that lived through and themselves remember the war years, than by the post-war generations whose approach is more historical. Confronted by this generational conflict, we are grateful to all those whose contributions serve to clarify the debate. Neither acts of injustice committed in the past nor the boundless suffering must sink into oblivion. It is necessary to extract a moral lesson with which to address the future so that such atrocities can never recur.

Our country, completely encircled by National Socialist and Fascist dictatorships, found itself in a precarious situation. Without complying with the totalitarian demands of her neighbors, Switzerland was nevertheless forced to make some compromises. In particular, Switzerland did not welcome as many refugees as she could have done so that the goods and fortunes of the victims and the persecuted could flow into Switzerland, permitting certain people to enrich themselves. We would like to evoke aspects of the past which reflect positively on our image. But we must also remind ourselves of the darker aspects of our history and accept the responsibility. We have inherited this past and have benefited from it. This enables us to be conscious of our obligations to make amends and to be ever vigilant in the face of the possibility of similar dangers, in the present or future, which now affects the manner in which we treat refugees or our responsibility with respect to acts of injustice.

At the time of Hitler's dictatorship and during the Second World War, unimaginable atrocities were committed, causing innumerable victims. The majority of these were the Jewish people, the designated target of the Holocaust. Indeed, this massacre was organized by a regime which also persecuted Christians and the churches. But we must not lose the perspective that, for centuries, Christians and ecclesiastical teachings were guilty of persecuting and marginalizing Jews, thus giving rise to antisemitic sentiments. Today, we shamefully declare that religious motivations, at that time, played a definite role in this process, motivations which are today largely incomprehensible. It is in reference to these pact acts of churches for which we proclaim ourselves culpable and ask pardon of the descendants of the victims, as the Holy Father has done in preparation for the Year of Reconciliation (cf. *Tertio Millennion Adveniente*, nos. 33 and 36).

Being aware of our responsibility for the facts of our past, we consider it to be our obligation to affirm that Christianity has grown out of Judaism and that consequently, the Christian faith is rooted in the Jewish tradition. In the face of National Socialist antisemitism, Pope Pius XI declared: "Through Christ and in Christ, we are the spiritual descendants of Abraham. Spiritually, we are all Semites" (cf *La Documentation Catholique*, 1938, col. 1460). The Second Vatican Council emphasized that "the Jewish people still remain most dear to God because of their fathers, for he does not repent of the gifts he makes nor of the calls he issues... His grace and his call are irrevocable. In company with the prophets and the same Apostle, the Church awaits that day, known to God alone, on which all people will address the lord in a single voice..." (*Nostra Aetate*, no. 4). Their psalms are our prayers, through which we raise our concerns before God.

With the National Council of the Christian Churches, our position is to affirm that "antisemitism and the Christian faith are incompatible. The churches in Switzerland resolutely distance themselves from all antisemitic affirmations." We wish, through our Commission of Judeo-Roman Catholic Dialogue, to find the ways best suited to implant this consciousness better in the life of the Church.

Declaration of Repentance

French Catholic Bishops
September 1997

As one of the major events of the twentieth century, the planned extermination of the Jewish people by the Nazis raises particularly challenging questions of conscience which no human being can ignore. The Catholic Church, far from wanting it to be forgotten, knows full well that conscience is formed in remembering, and that, just as no individual person can live in peace with himself, neither can society live in peace with a repressed or untruthful memory.

The Church of France questions itself. It, like the other churches, has been called to do so by Pope John Paul II as the third millennium draws near: "It is good that the Church should cross this threshold fully conscious of what she has lived through.... Recognizing the failing of yesteryear is an act of loyalty and courage which helps us strengthen our faith, which makes us face up to the temptations and difficulties of today and prepares us to confront them".

Following this year's celebration of the fiftieth anniversary of the Declaration of Seelisburg (that tiny village in Switzerland where, immediately after the war, on August 5, 1947, Jews and Christians drew up guidelines proposing a new understanding of Judaism) the undersigned bishops of France, because of the presence of internment camps in their dioceses, on the occasion of the forthcoming anniversary of the first statutes concerning the Jews drawn up by the Marechal Petain government (October 3, 1940), wish to take a further step. They do so in response to what their conscience, illuminated by Christ demands.

The time has come for the Church to submit her own history, especially that of this period, to critical examination and to recognize without hesitation the sins committed by members of the Church, and to beg forgiveness of God and humankind.

In France, the violent persecution did not begin immediately. But very soon, in the months that followed the 1940 defeat, antisemitism was sown at the state level, depriving French Jews of their rights and foreign Jews of their freedom. All of our national institutions were drawn into the application of these legal measures. By February 1941, some 40,000 Jews were in French internment camps. At this point, in a country which had been beaten, lay prostrate, and was partially occupied, the hierarchy saw the protection of its own faithful as its first priority, assuring as much as possible its own institutions. The absolute priority which was given to these objectives, in themselves legitimate, had the unhappy effect of casting a shadow over the biblical demand of respect for every human being created in the image of God.

This retreat into a narrow vision of the Church's mission was compounded by a lack of appreciation on the part of the hierarchy of the immense global tragedy which was being played out and which was a threat to Christianity's future. Yet many members of the Church and many non-Catholics yearned for the Church to speak out at a time of such spiritual confusion and to recall the message of Jesus Christ.

For the most part, those in authority in the Church, caught up in a loyalism and docility which went far beyond the obedience traditionally accorded civil authorities, remained stuck in conformity, prudence and abstention. This was dictated in part by their fear of reprisals against the Church's activities and youth movements. They failed to realize that the Church, called at that moment to play the role of defender within a social body that was falling apart, did in fact have considerable power and influence, and that in the face of the silence of other institutions, its voice could have echoed loudly by taking a definitive stand against the irreparable.

It must be borne in mind: During the occupation no one knew the full extent of the Hitlerian genocide. While it is true that mention could be made of a great number of gestures of solidarity, we have to ask ourselves whether acts of charity and help are enough to fulfill the demands of justice and respect for the rights of the human person.

So it is that, given the antisemitic legislation enacted by

the French government - beginning with the October 1940 law on Jews and that of June 1941, which deprived a whole sector of the French people of their rights as citizens, which hounded them out and treated them as inferior beings within the nation - and given the decision to put into internment camps foreign Jews who had thought they could rely on the right of asylum and hospitality in France, we are obliged to admit that the bishops of France made no public statements, thereby acquiescing by their silence in the flagrant violation of human rights and leaving the way open to a death-bearing chain of events.

We pass no judgment either on the consciences or on the people of that era; we are not ourselves guilty of what took place in the past; but we must be fully aware of the cost of such behavior and such actions. It is our Church, and we are obliged to acknowledge objectively today that ecclesiastical interests, understood in an overly restrictive sense, took priority over the demands of conscience—and we must ask ourselves why.

Over and above the historical circumstances which we already have recalled, we need to pay special attention to the religious reasons for this blindness. To what extent did secular antisemitism have and influence? Why is it, in the debates which we know took place, that the Church did not listen to the better claim of its members' voices? Before the war, Jacques Maritain, both in articles and in lectures, tried to open Christians up to a different perspective on the Jewish people. He also forcefully warned against the perversity of the antisemitism that was developing. Just before war broke out, Cardinal Saliege advised Catholics of the twentieth century to seek light in the teaching of Pius XI rather than in that of the thirteenth-century edicts of Innocent III. During the war, theologians and exegetes in Paris and in Lyons spoke out prophetically about the Jewish roots of Christianity, underlining how the shoot of Jesse flowered in Israel, that the two testaments were indissolubly linked, that the Virgin, Christ, and the apostles all were Jews, and that Christianity is linked to Judaism like a branch to the trunk that has borne it. Why was so little attention paid to such words?

Certainly, at a doctrinal level, the Church was fundamentally opposed to racism for the reasons, both theological and spiritual, which Pius XI expressed so strongly in his encyclical

Mit Brennender Sorge, which condemned the basic principles of National Socialism and warned Christians against the myth of race and of the all-powerful state. As far back as 1928, the Holy Office had condemned antisemitism. In 1938, Pius XI boldly declared, "Spiritually, we are all semites." But in the face of the constantly repeated anti-Jewish stereotypes, what weight could such condemnations carry? What weight could the thinking of theologians already referred to carry—thinking which can be found even after 1942 in statements which were not lacking in courage?

In the process which led to the *Shoah*, we are obliged to admit the role, indirect if not direct, played by commonly held anti-Jewish prejudices, which Christians were guilty of maintaining. In fact, in spite of (and to some extent because of) the Jewish roots of Christianity, and because of the Jewish people's fidelity throughout its history to the one God, the "original separation" dating back to the first century became a divorce, then an animosity, and ultimately a centuries-long hostility between Christians and Jews.

There can be no denying the weight of social, political, cultural and economic factors in the long story of misunderstanding and often of antagonism between Jews and Christians. However, one of the essential points in the debate was of a religious nature. This is not to say that a direct cause-and-effect link can be drawn between these commonly held anti-Jewish feelings and the *Shoah*, because the Nazi plan to annihilate the Jewish people has its sources elsewhere.

In the judgment of historians, it is a well-proven fact for centuries, up until Vatican Council II, an anti-Jewish tradition stamped its mark in differing ways on Christian doctrine and teaching, in theology, apologetics, preaching and in the liturgy. It was on such ground that the venomous plant of hatred for the Jews was able to flourish. Hence, the heavy inheritance we still bear in our century, with all its consequences which are so difficult to wipe out. Hence our still open wounds.

To the extent that the pastors and those in authority in the Church let such a teaching of disdain develop for so long, along with an underlying basic religious culture among Christian communities which shaped and deformed people's attitudes, they bear a grave responsibility. Even if they condemned antisemitic theories as being pagan in origin, they did not enlighten people's minds as they ought because they failed to call into question these centuries-old ideas and attitudes. This had a soporific effect on people's consciences, reducing their capacity to resist when the full violence of National Socialist antisemitism rose up, the diabolical and ultimate expression of hatred of the Jews, based on the categories of race and blood, and which was explicitly directed to the physical annihilation of the Jewish people. As Pope John Paul II put it, "an unconditional extermination... undertaken with premeditation".

Subsequently, when the persecution became worse and the genocidal policy of the Third Reich was unleashed within France itself, shared by the Vichy government, which put its own police force at the disposition of the occupier, some brace bishops raised their voices in a clarion call, in the name of human rights, against the rounding up of the Jewish population. These public statements, though few in number, were heard by many Christians.

Neither should the many actions undertaken by ecclesiastical authorities to save men, women, and children in danger of death be forgotten; nor the outpouring of Christian charity by the ordinary faithful, shown in generosity of every kind, often at great risk, in saving thousands and thousands of Jews.

Long before this, priest, religious, and lay people - some not hesitating to join underground movements - saved the honor of the Church, even if discreetly and anonymously. This also was done, in particular through the publication of *Les Cahiers du Temoignage Chretien* (Notebooks of Christian Witness), by denouncing in no uncertain terms the Nazi poison which threatened Christian souls with all its neopagan, racist, and antisemitic virulence, and by echoing the words of Pius XI: "Spiritually, we are all Semites". It is an established historical fact that the survival of a great number of Jews was assured thanks to such gestures of help from among Catholic and Protestant milieux, and by Jewish organizations.

Nevertheless while it may be true that some Christians—priest, religious and lay people—were not lacking in acts of courage in defense of fellow human beings, we must recognize that indifference won the day over indignation in the face of the persecution of the Jews and that, in particular, silence was the rule in face of the multifarious laws enacted by the Vichy government, whereas speaking out in favor of the victims was the exception.

As Francois Mauriac wrote, "A crime of such proportions falls for no small part on the shoulders of all those witnesses who failed to cry out, and this whatever the reason for their silence."

The end result is that the attempt to exterminate the Jewish people, instead of being perceived as a central question in human and spiritual terms, remained a secondary consideration. In the face of so great and utter a tragedy, too many of the Church's pastors committed an offense, by their silence, against the Church itself and its mission.

Today we confess that such a silence was a sin. In so doing, we recognize that the Church of France failed in her mission as teacher of consciences and that therefore she carries along with the Christian people the responsibility for failing to lend their aid, from the very first moments, when protest and protection were still possible as well as necessary, even if, subsequently, a great many acts of courage were performed.

This is the fact that we acknowledge today. For this failing of the Church of France and of her responsibility toward the Jewish people are part of our history. We confess this sin. We beg God's pardon, and we call upon the Jewish people to hear our words of repentance.

This act of remembering calls us to an ever keener vigilance on behalf of humankind today in the future.

Letter to the Jewish Community of Italy

Italian Bishops
March 1998
(The Italian Bishops' statement came in the form of a letter delivered to Professor Elio Toaff, the chief rabbi of Rome, and Dr. Tullia Zevi, the president of the Jewish Community of Italy.)

We have come to this place (the Great Synagogue of Rome), representatives of the Secretariat for Ecumenism and Dialogue of the Episcopal Conference of Italy. We wish our presence here to be a sign of friendship and hope: of our friendship toward you our "elder brothers," firstborn in the faith who have so much to tell us of the centuries-old treasure of biblical tradition; and of the hope that the maleficent plant of antisemitism will be extinguished forever from history, beginning with our cultural and linguistic habits.

In these days, we remember that one hundred and fifty years ago civil liberty was given by Carlo Alberto to the Waldensians and the Jews in his kingdom. It is a joyous memory in which we participate. But we also remember that sixty years ago racial laws were enacted against the Jews in Italy. This is a most painful memory that questions and disquiets us. "Antisemitism has no justification and is absolutely condemnable," John Paul II repeated for all with firmness and clarity on November 1, 1997, in his speech to the participants of the Vatican Symposium on the Relationship Between the Christians and Jews.

From our common biblical front we are fond of remembering in this regard two imperatives frequently used: *shema*, listen and *zechor*, remember; and one word without any equivocation, *teshuvah*, repentance.

It is true, as you have said, Rabbi Toaff, that "in Italy we had antisemitism of state not of the populace." But this does not take away from the fact that we deal with a dark page in the recent history of our country (the *Shoah*). Christian clergy for long centuries had cultivated "erroneous and unjust interpretations of scripture" (John Paul II, November 1, 1997). Because of this, we did not know how to muster energies capable of denouncing or to oppose with the necessary force and timeliness the iniquity that struck you.

However, spontaneous human charity and Christian solidarity with the Jewish people, and in particular of many priests and religious, did come to mitigate in some manner the lack of prophetic action when the situation passed from the violence of words to violence against persons. Yet such individual deeds were not sufficient to stop the catastrophe.

We recall these events with dismay and also with a profound and conscientious *teshuvah*. We do not want to, nor can we forget the victims. We remember them to learn and to hearken even more to the Eternal who loves life, the one Lord of all who knows our thoughts and acts. We resolve to be open to the full biblical truth, beginning with eminent dignity of humankind, upon which we reflected on this year's "Day of Solidarity with Judaism," January 17, 1998.

We recall with pleasure the initiative launched ten years ago by our secretariat to develop guidelines for the correct presentation of Judaism in preaching and catechesis. It has been received even on the European level. We proposed it in fact to the Ecumenical Assembly of Gratz last June before all the churches of Europe, achieving complete acceptance. On that occasion many were impressed by our firm position, as was stated of Professor Rene Samuel Sirat, chief rabbi of France, who was present. After unspeakable sufferings, truth has won over falsehood. Such a victory, however, is always fragile. It requires continual vigilance and permanent realization.

For its part, the Catholic Church, beginning with the Second Vatican Council—and thanks to the meeting of two men of faith, Jules Isaac and John XXIII, whose memory is a blessing - decisively turned in another direction, removing every pseudotheological justification for the accusation of deicide and perfidy and also the theory of substitution with its consequent "teaching of contempt," the foundation for all antisemitism. The Church recognizes with St. Paul that the gifts of God are irrevocable and that even today Israel has a proper mission to fulfill: to witness to the absolute lordship of the Most High, before whom the heart of every person must open.

In our times, what does our past ask of us? To recognize the truth, however painful, of the facts and of our responsibility. The Catholic Church in Italy shows clearly that it does not intend to exempt itself from this duty in spite of the delay, and despite some incautious voices still lingering over prejudices that have been hard to die out.

We leave to the historians the task of doing their best to reconstruct the truth of facts still drenched with emotion. As for you, only the Eternal knows through what iniquity and inhuman tribulation you have passed, remaining heroically faithful to your vocation as witnesses to God's name. For us it is asked to accelerate the removal of prejudices and injustices and to encourage esteem and respect; opening the mind and heart to the fraternity that unites us in the love of the one Lord and Father. It is a path of purification of remembrance for which we ask trust and good will. We ask as well the pardon of the Lord who is "slow to anger and abounding in steadfast love." (Ps 103:8)

It is a sign of reconciliation that we want to share. We are called to bear witness together in this our time, still so discordant and lacerated, to collaborate in the defense of liberty and justice and to secure civil and religious rights for all, beginning with our own country and everywhere among all peoples.

With these sentiments we are here to render homage, dear chief rabbi and president, to you, to your associates, to the rabbis, and to the members of the Italian Jewish community. We hope that our more positive relationship in the renewed context of civil and religious liberty will lead us to cooperate for the good of all in the anticipation of the kingdom.

We Remember: A Reflection on the Shoah

Holy See's Commission for Religious Relations with the Jews
March 1998

I. Tragedy of the *Shoah* and the Duty of Remembrance

The twentieth century is fast coming to a close, and a new millennium of the Christian era is about to dawn. The 2000th anniversary of the birth of Jesus Christ calls all Christians, and indeed invites all men and women, to seek to discern in the passage of history the signs of divine providence at work as well as the ways in which the image of the Creator in man has been offended and disfigured.

This reflection concerns one of the main areas in which Catholics can seriously take to heart the summons which Pope John Paul II has addressed to them in his apostolic letter *Tertio Millennio Advenente*:

> It is appropriate that as the second millennium of Christianity draws to a close the Church should become more fully conscious of the sinfulness of her children, recalling all those times in history when they departed from the spirit of Christ and his Gospel and, instead of offering to the world the witness of a life inspired by the values of faith, indulged in ways of thinking and acting which were truly forms of counter-witness and scandal. [162]

This century has witnessed an unspeakable tragedy which can never be forgotten: the attempt by the Nazi regime to exterminate the Jewish people, with the consequent killing of millions of Jews. Women and men, old and young, children and infants, for the sole reason of their Jewish origin, were persecuted and deported. Some were killed immediately, while others were degraded, ill-treated, tortured, and utterly robbed of their human dignity, and then murdered. Very few of those who entered the camps survived, and those who did remained scarred for life. This was the *Shoah*. It is a major fact of the history of this century, a fact which still concerns us today.

Before this horrible genocide, which the leaders of nations and Jewish communities themselves found hard to believe at the very moment when it was being mercilessly put into effect, no one can remain indifferent, least of all the Church, by reason of her very close bonds of spiritual kinship with the Jewish people and her remembrance of the injustices of the past. The Church's relationship to the Jewish people is unlike the one she shares with any other religion.[163] However, it is not only a question of recalling the past. The common future of Jews and Christians demands that we remember, for "there is no future without memory."[164] History itself is *memoria futuri*.

In addressing this reflection to our brothers and sisters of the Catholic Church throughout the world, we ask all Christians to join us in meditating on the catastrophe which befell the Jewish people and on the moral imperative to ensure that never again will selfishness and hatred grow to the point of sowing such suffering and death.[165] Most especially we ask our Jewish friends, "whose terrible fate has become a symbol of the aberrations of which man is capable when he turns against God,"[166] to hear us with open hearts.

II. What We Must Remember

While bearing their unique witness to the Holy One of Israel and to the Torah, the Jewish people have suffered much at different times and in many places. But the *Shoah* was certainly the worst suffering of all. The inhumanity with which the Jews were persecuted and massacred during this century is beyond the capacity of words to convey. All this was done to them for the sole reason that they were Jews.

The very magnitude of the crime raises many questions. Historians, sociologists, political philosophers, psychologists, and theologians are all trying to learn more about the reality of the *Shoah* and its causes. Much scholarly study still remains to be done. But such an event cannot be fully measured by the ordinary criteria of historical research alone. It calls for a "moral and religious memory" and, particularly among Christians, a very serious reflection on what gave rise to it.

The fact that the *Shoah* took place in Europe, that is, in countries of long standing Christian civilization, raises the question of the relation between the Nazi persecution and the attitudes down the centuries of Christians toward the Jews.

III. Relations Between Jews and Christians

The history of relations between Jews and Christians is a tormented one. His Holiness Pope John Paul II has recognized this fact in his repeated appeals to Catholics to see where we stand with regard to our relations with the Jewish people[167]. In effect, the balance of these relations over 2,000 years has been quite negative. [168]

At the dawn of Christianity, after the crucifixion of Jesus, there arose disputes between the early Church and the Jewish leaders and people who, in their devotion to the law, on occasion violently opposed the preachers of the Gospel and the first Christians. In the pagan Roman Empire, Jews were legally protected by the privileges granted by the emperor, and the authorities at first made no distinction between Jewish and Christian communities. Soon, however, Christians incurred the persecution of the state. Later, when the emperors themselves converted to Christianity, they at first continued to guarantee Jewish privileges. But Christian mobs who attacked pagan temples sometimes did the same to synagogues, not without being influenced by certain interpretations of the New Testament regarding the Jewish people as a whole.

"In the Christian world - I do not say on the part of the Church as such - erroneous and unjust interpretations of the New Testament regarding the Jewish people and their alleged culpability have circulated for too long, engendering feelings of hostility toward this people."[169] Such interpretations of the New Testament have been totally and definitively rejected by the Second Vatican Council.[170]

Despite the Christian preaching of love for all, even for one's enemies the prevailing mentality down the centuries penalized minorities and those who were in any way "different." Sentiments of anti-Judaism in some Christian quarters and the gap which existed between the Church and the Jewish people led to a generalized discrimination, which ended at times in expulsions or attempts at forced conversions. In a large part of the "Christian" world, until the end of the eighteenth century those who were not Christian did not always enjoy a fully guaranteed juridical status. Despite that fact, Jews throughout Christendom held on to their religious traditions and communal customs. They were therefore looked upon with a certain suspicion and mistrust. In times of crisis such as famine, war, pestilence or social tensions, the Jewish minority was sometimes taken as a scapegoat and became the victim of violence, looting, even massacres.

By the end of the eighteenth century and the beginning of the nineteenth century, Jews generally had achieved an equal standing with other citizens in most states and a certain number of them held influential positions in society. But in that same historical context, notably in the nineteenth century, a false and exacerbated nationalism took hold. In a climate of eventful social change, Jews were often accused of exercising an influence disproportionate to their numbers. Thus there began to spread in varying degrees throughout most of Europe an anti-Judaism that was essentially more sociological and political than religious.

At the same time, theories began to appear which denied the unity of the human race, affirming an original diversity of races. In the twentieth century, National Socialism in Germany used these ideas as a pseudoscientific basis for a distinction between so-called Nordic-Aryan races and supposedly inferior races. Furthermore, an extremist form of nationalism was heightened in Germany by the defeat of 1918 and the demanding conditions imposed by the victors, with the consequence that many saw in National Socialism a solution to their country's problems and cooperated politically with this movement.

The Church in Germany replied by condemning racism. The condemnation first appeared in the preaching of some of the clergy, in the public teaching of the Catholic bishops, and in the writings of lay Catholic journalists. Already in February and March 1931, Cardinal Bertram of Breslau, Cardinal Faulhaber and the bishops of Bavaria, the bishops of the province of Cologne, and those of the province of Freiburg published pastoral letters condemning National Socialism, with its idolatry of race and of the state.[171] The well-known Advent sermons of Cardinal Faulhaber in 1933, the very year in which National Socialism came to power, at which not just Catholics but also Protestants and Jews were present clearly expressed rejection of the Nazi antisemitic propaganda.[172] In the wake of the *Kristallnacht*, Bernard Lichtenberg, provost of Berlin cathedral, offered public prayers for the Jews. He was later to die at Dachau and has been declared blessed.

Pope Pius XI too condemned Nazi racism in a solemn way in his encyclical letter *Mit Brennender Sorge*,[173] which was read in German churches on Passion Sunday 1937, a step which resulted in attacks and sanctions against members of the clergy. Addressing a group of Belgian pilgrims on September 6, 1938, Pius XI asserted: "Antisemitism is unacceptable. Spiritually, we are all Semites."[174] Pius XII, in his very first encyclical, *Summi Pontificatus*[175] of October 20, 1939, warned against theories which denied the unity of the human race and against the deification of the state, all of which he saw as leading to a real "hour of darkness."[176]

IV. Nazi Antisemitism and The *Shoah*

Thus we cannot ignore the difference which exists between antisemitism, based on theories contrary to the constant teaching of the Church on the unity of the human race and on the equal dignity of all races and peoples, and the longstanding sentiments of mistrust and hostility that we call *anti-Judaism*, of which, unfortunately, Christians also have been guilty.

The National Socialist ideology went even further, in the sense that it refused to acknowledge any transcendent reality as the source of life and the criterion of moral good. Consequently, a human group, and the state with which it was identified, arrogated to itself absolute status and determined to remove the very existence of the Jewish people, a people called to witness to the one God and the law of the covenant. At the level of theological reflection we cannot ignore the fact that not a few in the Nazi Party not only showed aversion to the idea of divine providence at work in human affairs, but gave proof of a definite hatred directed at God himself.

Logically such an attitude also led to a rejection of Christianity and a desire to see the Church destroyed or a least subjected to the interests of the Nazi state.

It was this extreme ideology which became the basis of the measures taken first to drive the Jews from their homes and then to exterminate them. The *Shoah* was the work of a thoroughly modern neopagan regime. Its antisemitism had its roots outside of Christianity, and in pursuing its aims, it did not hesitate to oppose the Church and persecute her members also.

But it may be asked whether the Nazi persecution of the Jews was not made easier by the anti-Jewish prejudices imbedded in some Christian minds and hearts. Did anti-Jewish sentiment among Christians make them less sensitive or even indifferent to the persecutions launched against the Jews by National Socialism when it reached power?

Any response to this question must take into account that we are dealing with the history of people's attitudes and ways of thinking, subject to multiple influences. Moreover, many people were altogether unaware of the "final solution" that was being put into effect against a whole people; others were afraid for themselves and those near to them; some took advantage of the situation; and still others were moved by envy. A response would need to be given case by case. To do this, however, it is necessary to know what precisely motivated people in a particular situation.

At first the leaders of the Third Reich sought to expel the Jews. Unfortunately, the governments of some western countries of Christian tradition, including some in North and South America, were more than hesitant to open their borders to the persecuted Jews. Although they could not foresee how far the Nazi hierarchs would go in their criminal intentions, the leaders of those nations were aware of the hardships and dangers to which Jews living in the territories of the Third Reich were exposed. The closing of borders to Jewish emigration in those circumstances, whether due to anti-Jewish hostility or suspicion, political cowardice, or shortsightedness, or national selfishness, lays a heavy burden of conscience on the authorities in question.

In the lands where the Nazis undertook mass deportations, the brutality which surrounded these forced movements of helpless people should have led to suspect the worst. Did

Christians give every possible assistance to those being persecuted and in particular to the persecuted Jews?

Many did, but others did not. Those who did help to save Jewish lives, as much as was in their power, even to the point of placing their own lives in danger, must not be forgotten. During and after the war, Jewish communities and Jewish leaders expressed their thanks for all that had been done for them including what Pope Pius XII did personally or through his representatives to save hundreds of thousands of Jewish lives.[177] Many Catholic bishops, priests, religious, and laity have been honored for this reason by the state of Israel.

Nevertheless, as Pope John Paul II has recognized, alongside such courageous men and women, the spiritual resistance and concrete action of other Christians was not that which might have been expected from Christ's followers. We cannot know how many Christians in countries occupied or ruled by the Nazi powers or their allies were horrified at the disappearance of their Jewish neighbors and yet were not strong enough to raise their voices in protest. For Christians, this heavy burden of conscience of their brothers and sisters during the Second World War must be a call to penitence.[178]

We deeply regret the errors and failures of those sons and daughters of the Church. We make our own what is said in the Second Vatican Council's declaration *Nostra Aetate*, which unequivocally affirms: "The Church....mindful of her common patrimony with the Jews, and motivated by the gospel's spiritual love and by no political considerations, deplores the hatred, persecutions, and displays of antisemitism directed against the Jews at any time and from any source."[179]

We recall and abide by what Pope John Paul II, addressing the leaders of the Jewish community in Strasbourg in 1988, stated: "I repeat again with you the strongest condemnation of antisemitism and racism, which are opposed to the principles of Christianity."[180] The Catholic Church therefore repudiates every persecution against a people or human group any where, at any time. She absolutely condemns all forms of genocide as well as the racist ideologies which give rise to them. Looking back over this century, we are deeply saddened by the violence that has enveloped whole groups of peoples and nations. We recall in particular the massacre of the Armenians, the countless victims in Ukraine in the 1930s, the genocide of the Gypsies, which was also the result of racist ideas, and similar tragedies which have occurred in America, Africa, and the Balkans. Nor do we forget the millions of victims of totalitarian ideology in the Soviet Union, in China, Cambodia, and elsewhere. Nor can we forget the drama of the Middle East, the elements of which are well known. Even as we make this reflection, "many human beings are still their brothers' victims."[181]

V. Looking Together For A Common Future

Looking to the future of relations between Jews and Christians, in the first place we appeal to our Catholic brother and sisters to renew the awareness of the Hebrew roots of their faith. We ask them to keep in mind that Jesus was a descendant of David; that the Virgin Mary and the apostles belonged to the Jewish people; that the Church draws sustenance from the root of that good olive tree on to which have been grafted the wild olive branches of the gentiles (cf. Rom 11:17-24); that the Jews are our dearly beloved brothers, indeed in a certain sense they are "our elder brothers."[182]

At the end of this millennium the Catholic Church desires to express her deep sorrow for the failures of her sons and daughter in every age. This is an act of repentance (*teshuvah*), since as members of the Church we are linked to the sins as well as the merits of all her children. The Church approaches with deep respect and great compassion the experience of extermination, the *Shoah* suffered by the Jewish people during World War II. It is not a matter of mere words, but indeed of binding commitment. "We would risk causing the victims of the most atrocious deaths to die again if we do not have an ardent desire for justice, if we do not commit ourselves to ensure that evil does not prevail over good as it did for millions of the children of the Jewish people. ..... Humanity cannot permit all that to happen again."[183]

We pray that our sorrow for the tragedy which the Jewish people has suffered in our century will lead to a new relationship with the Jewish people. We wish to turn awareness of past sins into a firm resolve to build a new future in which there will be no more anti-Judaism among Christians or anti-Christian sentiment among Jews, but rather a shared mutual respect as befits those who adore the one Creator and Lord and have a common father in faith, Abraham.

Finally, we invite all men and women of good will to reflect deeply on the significance of the *Shoah*. The victims from their graves and the survivors through the vivid testimony of what they have suffered have become a loud voice calling the attention of all of humanity. To remember this terrible experience is to become fully conscious of the salutary warning it entails: the spoiled seeds of anti-Judaism and anti-semitism must never again be allowed to take root in any human heart.

March 16, 1998
Cardinal Edward Idris Cassidy, President
Bishop Pierre Duprey, Vice President
Rev. Remi Hoeckman, OP, Secretary

Notes

1. David Gerber, *Anti-Semitism in American History* (Chicago: University of Illinois Press, 1986), 3.

2. Philip A. Cunningham, *Education for Shalom* (Minnesota: The Liturgical Press, 1995), 39.

3. Benjamin W. Segel, *A LIE and A LIBEL: The History of the Protocols of the Elders of Zion* (Nebraska: Bison Books, 1995), 4.

4. Ibid., 56.

5. Ian Buruma, "War Guilt, and the Difference Between Germany and Japan," *New York Times* (29 December 1998).

6. Martilla and Kiley, "Survey on Anti-Semitism and Prejudice in America," (New York: Anti-Defamation League, October 1998).

7. J. Milton Yinger, *Anti-Semitism: A Case Study in Prejudice And Discrimination* (New York: Freedom Books, 1964), 5.

8. Sigmund Livingston, *Must Men Hate?* (Cleveland: World Publishing, 1945), xiv.

9. Walter Reich, "Erasing the Holocaust," *New York Times Book Review* (11 July 1993).

10. Robert S. Wistrich, *ANTISEMITISM: The Longest Hatred* (New York: Pantheon Books, 1991), xiv–xx.

11. Edward H. Flannery, *The Anguish of the Jews: Twenty-Three Centuries of Anti-Semitism* (New York: Macmillan, 1965), 288.

12. Ibid., 86.

13. Wistrich, op. cit., 24.

14. Simon R. Schwarzfuchs, *Encyclopaedia Judaica*, s.v. "Crusades" (Jerusalem: Keter, 1971), 5:1139.

15. Malcolm Hay, *The Roots of Christian anti-Semitism* (New York: Freedom Library Press, 1981), 19.

16. Ibid., xxiii.

17. "Church of the Creator" (New York: Anti-Defamation League, 1993).

18. Khalid Abdul Muhammad, Transcript [Speech] (19 February 1994).

19. Stuart Polly, "What Are the Protestants Teaching Their Teenagers about Jews and Judaism?" in *In Dialogue* (New York: Anti-Defamation League, 1994), 2:18–23.

20. Eric Greenberg, "Rewrite Not In The Works" Jewish Week (14 May 1999).

21. A. N. Wilson, *Jesus: A Life* (New York: Norton, 1992), 210.

22. Eugene J. Fisher, "Reflections on the Catechism of the Catholic Church" in *Interfaith Focus* (New York: Anti-Defamation League, 1994), vol. 1, no. 2, 16.

23. Eugene J. Fisher, "The Passion and Death of Jesus of Nazareth: Catechetical Approaches" in *Within Context: Essays on Jews and Judaism in the New Testament*, Efroymson, Fisher, and Klenicki, eds. (Minnesota: Liturgical Press, 1994), 112–113.

23a. Eugene J. Fisher and Rabbi Leon Klenicki, "Understanding the Jewish Experience" (New York: Anti-Defamation League and the Catholic Conference, Department of Education).

24. Abraham Duker, "Twentieth Century Blood Libels in the United States" in *The Blood Libel Legend*, ed., Allen Dundes (Madison: University of Wisconsin Press, 1991), 236–251.

25. Wistrich, op. cit., 207.

26. Duker, op. cit., 249–251.

26a. Encyclopedia Judaica, Volume 4, (Jerusalem: Keter Publishers, 1972), 1130.

26b. Abraham H. Foxman and Alan Schwartz, "Blood Libel: So Long Ago Yet So Near," Washington Jewish Week (22 October 1998).

27. "Poison in the Rap World," *New York Newsday*, Editorial (23 June 1989).

28. Tamar Levy, "Head of a UN Panel Makes it Known the Matzoh Zion Shall Not Rise," *Jewish Telegraphic Agency* (16 July 1991).

29. Kim Murphy, "Family Spy Case Deepens Distrust of Israel," *Los Angeles Times* (14 March 1992).

30. Khalid Abdul Muhammad, Transcript [Speech] from Kean College (29 November 1993).

30a. "1998 Audit of Anti-Semitic Incidents," Anti-Defamation League.

30b. Yaakov Galanti, "A Lesson in Anti-Semitism," Ma'ariv (6 May 1999).

31. Gavin I. Langmuir, *Toward a Definition of Antisemitism* (Berkeley: University of California Press, 1990), 13, 62.

32. Harold Fisch, ed., *The Holy Scriptures* (Jerusalem: Koren Publishers, 1980), 227.

33. "Japan and Anti-Semitism: The Proliferation of Anti-Jewish Literature," *ADL International Report* (New York: Anti-Defamation League, April 1987).

34. Robert Lenzner, "The End of the Line," *Sunday Boston Globe*, Business Section (18 August 1991).

35. "The Religious Right: The Assault on Tolerance and Pluralism in America," (New York: Anti-Defamation League, 1994).

36. Martin Kasendorf, "Brown Is Challenged on Choice of Jackson," *New York Newsday* (3 April 1992).

37. Muhammad, Kean Transcript, sup.

38. Gerald Krefetz, *Jews and Money: The Myths and the Reality* (New Haven: Ticknor and Fields, 1982), 54–63.

39. Bernard Glassman, *Anti-Semitic Stereotypes without Jews*, (Detroit: Wayne State University Press, 1975), 153–154.

40. ADL Incident Report (Boston: Anti-Defamation League, 1989).

41. *ADL In the Courts: Litigation Docket* (New York: Anti-Defamation League, Fall 1992), 39.

41a. "1998 Audit of Anti-Semitic Incidents," Anti-Defamation League.

42. David Singer, ed., *American Jewish Yearbook*, 1992 (New York: American Jewish Committee, 1992), 62.

43. Wistrich, op. cit., 127–128.

44. "The Protocols: Hoax of Hate" [Special Edition] (New York: Anti-Defamation League, June 1990).

45. Ibid.

46. Arnold Foster and Benjamin R. Epstein, *The New Anti-Semitism*, (New York: McGraw-Hill, 1972), 209.

47. "The Hamas Manifesto," *Congress Monthly* (New York: American Jewish Congress, March/April 1993), vol. 60, no. 3.

48. ADL Incident Report (Boston: Anti-Defamation League, 9 January 1992), no. 216.

49. "By Way of Deception Thou Shalt Do War," *National Vanguard* (West Virginia, January–February, 1992), 20.

49a. Louis Farrakhan, Transcript, Meet the Press [Interview], April 14, 1997.

50. "The Protocols: Hoax of Hate," op. cit.

51. Wistrich, op. cit., 6.

52. Livingston, op. cit., 50–57.

53. Lionel Kochan, ed., *The Jews in Soviet Russia since 1917* (New York: Oxford University, 1978), 322–323.

54. Gore Vidal, "The Empire Strikes Back," *Nation* (22 March 1986), 350–353.

55. "From Columnist to Candidate: Pat Buchanan's Religious War" (New York: Anti-Defamation League, 1992), 10.

56. Martilla Communications/Kiley & Company, "Highlights from a November 1998 ADL Survey on Anti-Semitism and Prejudice in America" (New York: Anti-Defamation League).

56a. Louis Farrakhan, Transcript, National Press Club [Speech], October 19, 1998.

57. Paul Mendes-Flohr and Jehuda Reinharz, *The Jew in the Modern World* (New York: Oxford University Press, 1980), 393–394.

58. William F. Buckley, Jr., *In Search of Anti-Semitism* (New York: Continuum Publishing, 1992), 44.

59. Deborah Lipstadt, *Denying the Holocaust* (New York: Free Press, 1993), 21.

60. Ibid., 15.

61. "Extremism on the Right" (New York: Anti-Defamation League, 1988), 36–37.

62. "Fred Leuchter, Jr." [Special Edition] (New York: Anti-Defamation League, October 1990), 31. (On June 12, 1991, Leuchter was charged with misrepresentation and sentenced to two years' probation.)

63. Bradley R. Smith, "The Holocaust Controversy: The Case for Open Debate" [Advertisement].

64. "Bradley Smith: A Man and His Myth" [Special Edition] (New York: Anti-Defamation League, February 1992).

65. Mendes-Flohr and Reinharz, op. cit., 508.

66. Ibid., 514.

66a. Israel Gutman (Editor-in-Chief), Encyclopedia of the Holocaust, Volume 2, New York, 1990, p. 657.

67. "Excerpts from Speech by German President," *New York Times* (9 May 1985).

68. *ADL On the Frontline*, "Decision of Student Editors to Accept or Reject Holocaust Revisionist Advertisement in University Newspapers [In brief] (New York: Anti-Defamation League, February–March 1994), 7, 1.

69. "Advertising Hate," *Boston Globe* (14 December 1993).

70. Thomas Robb, *White Patriot* [Klan Publication] (Arkansas, March 1998).

71. Cornel West, "Pride and Prejudice," *Time* (26 February 1994), 21–34.

72. Anthony Martin, *Blacks and Jews News* (Wellesley, Mass., Winter 1991)

73. *The Secret Relationship Between Blacks and Jews* (Boston: Historical Research Department of the Nation of Islam, 1991), 1:vii.

74. Anthony Martin, *Blacks and Jews at Wellesley News* [Broadside] (Wellesley, Mass., March 1993), no. 1.

75. Orlando Patterson, "Multicultural Education: Will Extremists Destroy the Dream?", *ADL Panel Program* (20 March 1992).

76. Saul Friedman, "An Old/New Libel: Jews In the Slave Trade," *Midstream* (October 1991).

77. Ibid., 13.

78. David Brion Davis, "The Slave Trade and the Jews," *New York Review of Books* (22 December 1994), 15.

79. Henry Louis Gates [Letter] (9 February 1992).

80. Selwyn R. Cudjoe, *Wellesley News* (3 March 1993).

81. *The Secret Relationship Between Blacks and Jews*, op. cit.

82. Abraham H. Foxman, "Jew Hatred as History: An Analysis of the Nation of Islam's *The Secret Relationship Between Blacks and Jews*," 1st ed. (New York: Anti-Defamation League, 1993), 1.

83. Ibid.

84. Anthony Martin, *The Jewish Onslaught: Despatches from the Wellesley Battlefront* (Dover, Mass.: Majority Press, 1993), 35.

85. Anthony Martin, Transcript [Speech] from Howard University (April 1994).

86. *The Final Call* (Chicago, 11 June 1996).

87. Selwyn R. Cudjoe, "Academic Responsibility and Black Scholars," *Baltimore Sun* (23 March 1994).

88. David Aaron, *Journal of the American Academy of Religion* (Winter 1995), vol. 63, no. 4, 721–759.

89. Ibid.

90. Ibid.

91. 42 U.S.C. s 2000e-(j)

92. Boston Globe, July 27, 1992.

94. Flannery, op. cit., 4.

95. Benzion Netanyahu, *The Origins of the Inquisition in Fifteenth-Century Spain* (New York: Random House, 1995), 24

96. Mary C. Boys, "A More Faithful Portrait of Judaism: An Imperative for Christian Education," in David Efroymsin, Eugene J. Fisher, and Leon Klenicki, eds., *Within Context: Essays on Jews and Judaism in the New Testament* (Collegeville, Minn.: Liturgical Press, 1993), 4.

97. Ibid., 5.

98. Clark M. Williamson and Ronald J. Allen, *Interpreting Difficult Texts: Anti-Judaism and Christian Preaching* (Philadelphia: Trinity Press International, 1989), 3–6.

99. Most of what Isaac designates as "anti-Semitism" falls under the definition of anti-Judaism in this work.

100. Jules Isaac, *Has Anti-Semitism Christian Roots?* (New York: National Conference on Christians and Jews, 1962), 77–85

101. Christopher Leighton, cited in Norman Beck, *Mature Christianity in the Twenty-First Century* (New York: Crossroad, 1994), 24.

102. Ibid., 24 f.

103. Roy A. Eckardt, cited in James Charlesworth, ed., *Jews and Christians Exploring the Past, Present, and Future* (New York: Crossroad, 1990), 164.

104. Bernhard Olsen, cited in Isaac, *Has Anti-Semitism Christian Roots?*, 11 ff.

105. Eliezer Berkovits, cited in Beck, *Mature Christianity*, 30.

106. Eckardt, cited in Charlesworth, *Jews and Christians*, 163.

107. Olsen, cited in Isaac, *Has Anti-Semitism Christian Roots?*, 23

108. Norman Solomon, cited in Leon Klenicki, ed., *Toward a Theological Encounter: Jewish Understandings of Christianity* (New York: Paulist Press, 1991), 32.

109. The reference to "strenuous effort" should not obscure the insight that it is also in gentle effort that much is accomplished.

110. Abraham Heschel, cited in Samuel Dresner, ed., *I Asked for Wonder* (New York: Schocken Books, 1991) 40 f.

111. For an expert discussion of the "classic," see David Tracy, *Blessed Rage for Order* (New York: Seabury Press, 1975), chaps. 1 and 2.

112. See Sandra Schneiders, *Women and the Word: Gender of God in the New Testament* (New York: Paulist, 1984), 38.

113. For a clear discussion of the evolution of belief regarding Jesus Christ in first- and second-century Christianity, see Richard P. McBrien, *Catholicism* (San Francisco: Harper, 1981), 373–75.

114. Charlesworth, op. cit., 37.

115. Philip Cunningham, cited in Efroymson, Fisher, and Klenicki, *Within Context*, 64.

116. Daniel J. Harrington, "The Problem of 'the Jews' in John's Gospel," *Exploration* 8 (1994), no. 1:2.

117. Ibid., 3.

118. Charlesworth, op. cit., 50.

119. Harrington, "The Problem," 3 f.

120. Ibid., 3.

121. Krister Stendahl, *Paul Among Jews and Gentiles* (Philadelphia: Fortress Press, 1976), 4.

122. Ibid., 7.

123. Ibid.

124. Harrington, "The Problem," 3.

125. Charlesworth, op. cit., 37.

126. Eugene Borowitz, *Contemporary Christologies: A Jewish Response* (New York: Paulist Press, 1980), 179.

127. James Charlesworth, "Philo: The Jewish Genius of Alexandria," *Explorations* 8 (1994), no. 1:2.

128. Eugene J. Fisher, "The Passion and Death of Jesus of Nazareth: Catechetical Approaches," in Efroymson, Fisher, and Klenicki, eds., *Within Context*, 114.

129. Leon Klenicki and Eugene J. Fisher, *Roots and Branches: Biblical Judaism, Rabbinic Judaism, and Early Christianity* (Winona, Minn.: St. Mary's Press, 1987), 18.

130. Ibid., 15.

132. Fisher, "The Passion and Death," 115.

132. Krister Stendahl, "Anti-Semitism and the New Testament," *Explorations* 7 (1993), no. 2:7.

133. Flannery, *Anguish of the Jews*, 3.

134. Ibid., 38

135. Franklin Littell, *The Crucifixion of the Jews* (Detroit: Wayne State University Press, 1975), 27

136. Ibid., 28

137. Williamson and Allen, op. cit., 7.

138. Jacob Neusner, *Jews and Christians: The Myth of a Common Tradition* (London: SCM, 1991), 199.

139. Ambrose, cited in Williamson and Allen, op. cit., 16.

140. Chrysostom, cited in Rosemary Ruether, *Faith and Fratricide: The Christian Theological Roots of Anti-Semitism* (New York: Seabury Press, 1974), 146 f.

141. Augustine, 'Reply to Faustus the Manichean,' cited in Boys, op. cit., 6.

142. Augustine, "Reply," cited in Leon Klenicki, ed., *Toward a Theological Encounter: Jewish Understanding of Christianity* (New York: Paulist Press), 2.

143. Flannery, op. cit., 255.

144. Ruether, op. cit., 195.

145. Ibid., 213 ff.

146. Martin Luther, "The Jews and Their Lies," in Gerhard Falk, *The Jews in Christian Theology* (Jefferson, N.C.: McFarland Press, 1992), 432.

147. Jules Isaac, *The Teaching of Contempt: Christian Roots of Anti-Semitism* (New York: Holt, Rinehart & Winston, 1964), 24.

148. Flannery, op. cit., 258.

149. Ibid., 258 ff.

150. Davis S. Wyman, *The Abandonment of the Jews* (New York: Pantheon Books, 1984), 10 ff.

151. Christian Scholars' Group on Judaism and the Jewish People—Catholic Membership, "Statement on the Catechism of the Catholic Church," *Professional Approaches for Christian Educator* (PACE) 24 (September 1994):43 f.

152. Joseph Ratzinger, "Reconciling the Gospel and Torah: The Catechism," *Origins* 23 (February 24, 1994), no. 36:623.

153. William H. Wilimon, "What Bible Are Your Children Reading?" *Explorations* 7, no. 1 (1993):1.

154. ADL, "Farrakhan Unchanged: The Continuing Message of Hate" (New York: Anti-Defamation League, 1994), 15.

155. ADL, "Holocaust Denial" (New York: Anti-Defamation League, 1994), 8 f.

156. Eugene J. Fisher, *Anti-Semitism Is a Sin* (Washington, D.C.: United States Catholic Conference, 1990), 5.

157. Philip Cuningham, "Jews and Judaism in Catholic Religion Textbooks: Progress, Problems, and Recommendations," *Professional Approaches for Christian Educators* (PACE) 22 (December 1992):17–21

158. Williamson and Allen, op. cit., 6 f.

159. Norman Solomon, "Themes in Christian-Jewish Relations," in Klenicki, *Theological Encounters*, 31.

160. Klenicki, *Theological Encounters*, 70.

161. Heschel, "What Is Ecumenism?", 2.

162. John Paul II, apostolic letter *Tertio Millennio Adveniente Acta Apostolicae Sedis*(AAS)87 (1995): 25, no. 33.

163. Cf. John Paul II, speech at the Rome synagogue, April 13, 1986. AAS 78 (1986):1120, no. 4.

164. John Paul II, Angelus prayer, June 11, 1995. *Insegnamenti* 18/1 (1995): 1712.

165. Cf. John Paul II, address to Jewish leaders in Budapest, August 18, 1991. *Insegnamenti* 14/7 (1991):349, no. 4.

166. John Paul II, encyclical *Centesimus Annus*. AAS 83 (1991): 814-815 , no. 17.

167. Cf. John Paul II address to episcopal conference delegates for Catholic-Jewish relations, March 6, 1982. *Insegnamenti* 5/1 (1982): 743-747.

168. Cf. Holy See's Commission for Religious Relations with the Jews, *Notes on the Correct Way to Present the Jews and Judaism in Preaching and Catechesis in the Roman Catholic Church*, June 24, 1985, VI 1. Enchiridion Vaticanum 9, 1656.

169. Cf. Joh Paul II, speech to symposium on the roots of Anti-Judaism, October 31, 1997. *L'Osservatore Romano* (November 1, 1997): 6, no. 1.

170. Cf. Vatican Council II *Nostra Aetate*, no. 4.

171. Cf. B. Statiewski, ed., *Akten Deutscher Bischofe Uber die Lage der Kirche*, 1933-1945, Vol. I, 1933-1934 (Mainz, 1968), Appendix.

172. Cf. L. Volk, *Der Bayerische Episkopat und der Nationalisozialismus 1930-1934* (Mainz, 1966), 170-174.

173. The encyclical is dated March 14, 1937. AAS 29 (1937): 145-167.

174. *La Documentation Catholique*, 29 (1938): col 1460

175. AAS 31 (1939): 413-453

176. Ibid., 449

177. The wisdom of Pope Pius XII's diplomacy was publicly acknowledged on a number of occasions by representative Jewish organizations and personalities. For example, on September 7, 1945, Dr. Joseph Nathan, who represented the Italian Hebrew Commission, stated: "Above all, we acknowledge the supreme pontiff and the religious men and women who, executing the directives of the Holy Father, recognized the persecuted as their brother and, with efforts and abnegation, hastened to help us, disregarding the terrible dangers to which they were exposed" (*L'Osservatore Romano*[September 8, 1945]: 2). On September 21 of that same year, Pius XII received in audience Dr. A. Leo Kubowitzki, secretary general of the World Jewish Congress, who came to present "to the Holy Father, in the name of the Union of Israelitic Communities, warmest thanks for the efforts of the Catholic Church on behalf of Jews throughout Europe during the war" (*L'Obsservatore Romano*) [September 23, 1945]:1). On Thursday, November 29, 1945, the

pope met about eighty representatives of Jewish refugees from various concentration camps in germany, who expressed "their great honor at being able to thank the Holy Father personally for his generosity toward those persecuted during the Nazi-Fascist period" (*L'Osservatore Romano*) [November 30, 1945]:1). In 1958, at the death of Pope Pius XII, Golda Meir sent an eloquent message: "We share in the grief of humanity. When fearful martyrdom came to our people, the voice of the pope was raised for its victims. The life of our times was enriched by a voice speaking out about great moral truths above the tumult of daily conflict. We mourn a great servant of peace".

178. Cf. John Paul II, address to the Federal German Republic's new ambassador to the Holy See, November 8, 1990. AAS 83 (1991): 587-588, no. 2.

179. *Nosta Aetate*, no. 4. Translation by Walter M. Abbott, SJ, in *The Documents of Vatican II*.

180. John Paul II, address to Jewish leaders in Strasbourg, October 9, 1988. Insegnamenti 11/3 (1988):1134, no. 8.

181. John Paul II, address to the diplomatic corps, January 15, 1994. AAS 86 (1994):816, no. 9.

182. John Paul II, Rome synagogue speech, no. 4.

183. John Paul II, address at a commemoration of the *Shoah*, April 7, 1994. *Insegnamenti* 17/1 (1994): 897 and 893, no. 3.

Bibliography

Audit of Anti-Semitic Incidents, Copyright 1999, ADL.

Dundes, Alan, ed. *The Blood Libel Legend*. Madison: University of Wisconsin Press, 1991.

Flannery, Edward H. *The Anguish of the Jews: Twenty-Three Centuries of Anti-Semitism*. New York: Macmillan, 1965.

Foster, Arnold. *Square One*. New York: Donald I. Fine, 1988.

Glassman, Bernard. *Anti-Semitic Stereotypes Without Jews*. Detroit: Wayne State University Press, 1975.

Grosser, Paul E., and Edwin G. Halpern. *The Causes and Effects of Anti-Semitism*. New York: The Philosophical Library, 1978.

Gould, Alan, ed. *What Did They Think of the Jews?* Northvale, N.J.: Jason Aronson, 1991.

Hay, Malcolm. *The Root of Christian Anti-Semitism*. New York: Freedom Library Press, 1981.

Krefets, Gerald. *Jews and Money*. New Haven: Ticknor & Fields, 1982.

Langmuir, Gavin, I. *Toward A Definition of Antisemitism*. Berkeley: University of California Press, 1990.

Lipstadt, Deborah E. *Denying The Holocaust: The Growing Assault on Truth and Memory*. New York: Free Press, 1993.

Livingston, Sigmund. *Must Men Hate?* Cleveland: World Publishing, 1945.

Mendes-Flohr, Paul R., and Jehuda Reinharz. *The Jew in the Modern World*. New York: Oxford University Press, 1980.

Prager, Dennis and Joseph Telushkin. *Why the Jews? The Reason for Anti-Semitism*. New York: Simon and Schuster, 1983.

Trachtenberg, Joshua. *The Devil and the Jews*. New Haven: Yale University Press, 1943.

Wistrich, Robert S. *ANTISEMITISM: The Longest Hatred*. New York: Pantheon Books, 1991.